DISCOVERING DYSCALCULIA

One family's journey with a math disability

Laura M. Jackson

GHF Press

Discovering Dyscalculia
One family's journey with a math disability

Editor: Ann Grahl
Interior design: Sztrecska Publishing
Cover design: David Provolo

Published by GHF Press, an imprint of GHF Learners
ghflearners.org

ISBN: 978-1-7375161-2-5

Dedication

For dyscalculics everywhere—
may you feel seen, understood,
and empowered.

Contents

Acknowledgments

Becoming a writer and published author is a new and unexpected part of my personal journey. While a box in my closet containing journals from the age of 13 until the birth of my first child may suggest otherwise, I never considered myself a writer—until recently.

Over two years ago, our family made a pivotal move from our beloved city home of 15 years to a quiet location just outside the city. This new home in the woods with its peaceful beauty is where I began working through Julia Cameron's *The Artist's Way*, uncovering my blocked inner artist and freeing creative parts of myself that had been dormant. I began writing the recommended "morning pages"—three pages longhand in a notebook every morning. In the process, new areas of creativity began to emerge. One was blogging on my new website, *Discovering Dyscalculia*, which would end up being discovered by an editor who asked if I'd consider writing a book. I was caught off-guard and shied away at first. But, with coaxing from my husband and the words in *The Artist's Way*, I decided to take the plunge and open myself to this new adventure.

There are so many wonderful individuals to thank for their help in the writing process as well as in our particular journey with dyscalculia. I am grateful:

To my friend Courtney Grager, who first shared the idea of a math learning disability with me and who continues to send me encouraging emails and cheer me on in my advocacy work.

To my daughter's teachers—Lara Francisco, Devin Liner, Julie Colando, and Julia Manno—who were kind, patient, and open to learning how to help my daughter.

To the authors and educational experts whose knowledge of dyscalculia and advocacy work have been a priceless gift—Dorian Yeo, Brian Butterworth, Jane Emerson, Patricia Babtie, Ronit Bird, A.M. Schreuder, Samantha Abeel, Catherine Eadle, and Robert Jennings.

To all the parents of dyscalculic children, teachers, dyscalculic adults, friends, and family, who read my weekly emails about dyscalculia and whose positive response and feedback keep me writing.

To Julia Cameron, for inspiring me to put pen to paper for my daily morning pages, for reigniting my passion for writing, and for helping me heal and rediscover my own inner artist.

To Jeff and Marit Krueger, whose beautiful island home is where I began writing again.

To Nikki Hegstrom, former GHF press editor, who reached out and asked if I would write a book.

To my current GHF editor, Ann Grahl, who put in many hours during a global pandemic to work on this project, guiding a newbie through the process.

To Lacey Redinger, for pouring over book cover designs with me and for her enthusiastic support.

To the "Artist's Way Gals," my friends Lisa Call, Linda-Jo Duffy, and Kathy Hatch, who walked with me through the ongoing process of becoming aware of my artistic blocks, gently encouraging me to be myself and celebrating each success.

To my therapist, for the consistent support and help navigating my inner world and for the encouragement to extend myself greater compassion and to celebrate this accomplishment.

To my two daughters, who supported and flexed when I was away working on the book and when I was with them in body but lost in thought. To Quinn, for sharing her keen eye for detail. It's not easy when your mom writes a book connected to your sister's learnings struggles and you feel left out. Know that you are so very special, unique, and loved, even if I haven't written a book about you, yet. I see you and love you dearly. To my daughter Emma. I wouldn't have written this book without you and our experience learning more about this unique part of you. Thank you for being willing to share your story with others and for your positive words of encouragement to write our story. I love you dearly.

To my husband and best friend, Sean, who continually cheers me on; provides space for me to write; and reads, edits, and suggests revisions for all my writing. You have been my closest confidant and constant source of support. I couldn't have written this book or pursued any of the creative ventures of the past few years without your supportive presence. Thank you for helping me step out more bravely into new things. I love you so very much.

To the Great Creator, who continues to draw me into more freedom, abundance, and possibility than I could ever imagine.

Introduction

As our family's journey into the world of dyscalculia began, we often found ourselves confused and anxious. While it was slightly comforting to discover a possible reason for my daughter's struggle with numbers and math, it was extremely difficult to find information about this specific learning disability. In the hours spent scouring the internet, I came across very little that aided my understanding of dyscalculia, let alone any resources on how to best support my daughter as she faced this challenge.

I wondered why so little was known about this learning disability when it impacts 3–8% of the population. Where was the educational curriculum for students with dyscalculia? Why could I not find any blogs or online articles from parents who had navigated their child's dyscalculia? The void of information and support was not just online; it was also difficult to find a teacher or parent in our community who had even heard of dyscalculia.

Almost five years later, I find myself with more understanding and a growing knowledge about dyscalculia, which has freed our family from the confusion and anxiety that we initially felt. It has been a deeply rewarding process to learn more about my daughter's unique way of experiencing numbers and calculations. We now have a common language to communicate about her dyscalculia and have acquired valuable tools to help her succeed in school and life.

During the beginning of the COVID-19 pandemic in 2020, I began blogging about our experience with dyscalculia. I hoped the blog would be a resource for other parents like myself, as well as a creative outlet for me to process our story. Shortly after I began, a GHF Press editor contacted me and asked if I would be interested in writing a book on dyscalculia. After taking some time to deal with my imposter syndrome, I said "yes." And I agreed to author the kind of book I had searched for at the start of my family's journey.

This book is for parents who have a child struggling in math and wonder if a learning disability is the cause, as well as for parents whose child has received a dyscalculia diagnosis and who are curious about next steps. I have included many personal stories detailing moments of frustration and also the "aha!" moments of success on our winding road of discovering dyscalculia.

Some of the topics covered in this volume include the following:

- Recognizing the signs and symptoms of dyscalculia
- Public school versus private evaluations
- Common obstacles with assessments and special education
- Best alternatives to help dyscalculic students learn
- Methods to alleviate anxiety
- Practical help for everyday life
- Advocating for your child

This book will contribute to a greater understanding and awareness of the impact of dyscalculia. You will find you are not alone in the angst or bewilderment you may be facing. You will gain a growing knowledge of what a dyscalculic child needs to thrive and where to get the support your child needs.

As a parent on a similar journey, I can personally attest that there is a light at the end of what may feel like a long and dark tunnel. I am happy to accompany you on this trek as a fellow traveler and advocate.

chapter 1

Discovery

It was not until our daughter was 10 years old that we discovered she had a math learning disability. Up to that point, I had figured my daughter was simply not interested in math and that her math comprehension would grow in time. She had so many other interests and was a lively, curious, and imaginative child.

However, near the middle of third grade, I began to wonder about her math struggles. She was now nine years old and having noticeable difficulty in math class. She was increasingly exhausted after school and began to talk about how much she hated math. Even with extra help from the math specialist a few times a week, she was falling behind the rest of the class and returning home daily with unfinished classwork. When we sat down to complete the worksheets, it was evident that she did not understand the material, and what she did understand she completed very slowly.

My daughter especially dreaded the weekly multiplication drills when all the students would complete as many multiplication facts as they could on a repeated drill sheet. As the months went by, her progress on the drills did not improve. She could only complete the "0" and "1" times tables and some of the "2" times table, while her classmates were able to complete most or all of the problems.

There had been some hints of difficulty with math before the third grade. In second grade, the school suggested she receive additional help from the school's math specialist. These sessions with the math specialist occurred outside of class a few times a week and continued through second and third grades. During the summer before third grade, there had been tears and much anxiety when we attempted to use flashcards for addition and subtraction fluency. My daughter knew that the sum of $4 + 2$ was 6, but when I showed her the next card in the same grouping of numbers, $6 - 2 =$ _, she squirmed and had no idea what the answer was. The flashcards caused so much anxiety that we eventually gave up using them.

I was confused by the discrepancy between her curiosity and love for learning and how she was performing in math class. She seemed so bright. However, even with the extra help she was receiving from the math specialist, she was not making the progress that was expected. Were we not doing enough? Was she not trying hard enough? What were we missing? The continued math struggles were impacting our daughter's confidence and causing a growing amount of anxiety. At a particularly low point, she tearfully asked, "Mommy, am I stupid?"

Not long after my daughter voiced this distressing query, a lunch conversation with a friend brought about a possibility I had not considered.

It had been a sunny but cold winter afternoon when I sat down with my friend for a weekday lunch and visit. We chatted about the latest news in each other's lives. My friend had inquired about how my girls were doing. She had a special connection to them, as she had raised two daughters herself. Because it was on my mind, I shared with her the issues my elder daughter was having in math. My friend listened and nodded with understanding. She told me that she had also struggled in math and shared how she barely made it through her college math exams because of her math learning disability.

"A *math* learning disability?" I asked. I had never heard of a learning disability in math. In fact, the idea of a learning disability had never crossed my mind as a possible reason for my daughter's math troubles.

After we finished lunch and I had closed the front door, I grabbed my laptop to search for "math learning disability." The first informative site I found was *Understood.org*. While the website was not nearly as robust as it is now (in 2021), there was a small section on a math learning disability called "dyscalculia."

I remember looking at the list of symptoms and feeling a flood of emotions as I read. The description of someone with dyscalculia matched my daughter perfectly.

I was initially bewildered. Why had I never heard of this? Why was this possibility never brought up by her teachers? Why had I never heard any parents talk about this in any of the many parenting circles I was involved in? Why had I never read any books or articles about this?

Embarrassment and regret followed. I could recall many times I had assumed my daughter was not trying hard enough, was not focused, or was being lazy. I had assumed it was something within her control to change and she was choosing not to. Here, I could see that I had been making many inaccurate and even harmful assumptions.

Relief was also present. There was almost a wave of excitement at this new knowledge. Finally, maybe there was a real reason for all the confusing struggles we were facing. Maybe there were some answers to be found and some help to be given.

As I continued to research, I began to recognize that so many of my daughter's specific struggles could be explained as symptoms of dyscalculia.

What is Dyscalculia?

Dyscalculia is a learning disability that impacts one's ability to access and apply mathematical skills. It is a fundamental difference in how a person experiences numbers, and it impacts their learning and understanding of math concepts. Dyscalculia is not a result of poor teaching methods, lack of education, or low intelligence. Like most learning disabilities, one is born with dyscalculia. This learning disability is estimated to impact somewhere between 3 and 8% of the world's population, yet it is much lesser known and understood than other learning disabilities. Sometimes, the phrases *math learning disability* or *a specific learning disability with an impairment in mathematics* will be used to describe dyscalculia.

The Signs and Symptoms of Dyscalculia

The signs and symptoms of dyscalculia all point to a lack of number sense. Dyscalculics lack a basic understanding of and feeling for numbers and what they represent.

Someone with dyscalculia will have difficulty with the ordinary numerical operations of addition, subtraction, multiplication, and division. It is common for a dyscalculic student to make their way through the lower grades in school without their learning disability being detected because they can count reliably well by ones and do simple addition. However, when they begin learning the operations of subtraction, multiplication, and division, the difficulty with performing these numerical operations becomes apparent.

Subtraction, even with very small numbers, can be especially difficult for dyscalculics. For example, when playing a simple math game, my daughter would be unable to work out $8 - 3 = \_$. Sometimes, she would solve a subtraction problem by using a method she could understand, which was counting upward from zero. If the question was $10 - 6 = \_$, she would solve this by drawing 10 dots with her pencil. Then, she would cross off 6 dots, starting with zero and counting up to 6. She would then begin back at zero and individually count up how many dots were not crossed off to arrive at the answer "4," 10 − 6 = 4. She could not conceptualize the idea of removing 6 from 10 and knowing how many would be left. This difficulty with subtraction continued as she grew older. Recently, she was completely stumped by the problem 20 − 6 = _. She spent a great deal of time trying to come up with various ways she could solve this problem. After puzzling over it for several minutes, even wondering if her times table songs might help her solve it, she moved on, unable to find the answer.

For dyscalculic learners, it is difficult to count by any method other than counting by ones, including counting backward, skip counting, or sequencing numbers from various starting points. The average person learns to access a number line in their mind to help them perform basic counting skills by moving up and down that number line. Dyscalculics do not have this natural number line easily accessible in their minds. This is one reason they may be able to move up the number line for addition by ones but become lost if asked to count backward or to subtract one or two numbers from another. Even now my daughter will become visibly stressed when asked to count backward. The work requires much concentration, especially when the tens column changes, for example, when counting from the number 40 backward to the number 39.

Learning to skip count was very difficult for my daughter until we began using songs to help her memory. Still, she had to start at the beginning of each song to remember the particular order of the numbers and was unable to randomly pull the related multiplication facts out from the song.

Finger-counting can be a sign of dyscalculia. Often a dyscalculic student will calculate with their fingers inconspicuously because they notice their peers no longer use this method of calculation. Finger-counting itself is not a sign of dyscalculia unless it seems to be the only reliable counting method available to the person, which could mean that they have been unable to grasp more efficient strategies of calculation.

Most dyscalculics are unable to subitize. To subitize is to automatically see small quantities and know the total quantity without counting. This ability can be observed in children at a young age. However, for dyscalculics, this skill is not innate and needs to be explicitly taught. While playing dice games, a dyscalculic student will most likely count each individual dot on a die to determine the count. Adding two dice would require counting by ones on the first die and then continuing to count by ones on the second die. Or, you may ask a dyscalculic friend how many family members are seated at the table and notice that they count each person individually instead of quickly seeing there are only five family members seated.

Recently, my daughter and I were working with a string of 100 beads that were divided by tens; each group of 10 was a different color. She had created the string of beads during a previous math lesson. For this lesson, I asked her to find the 28th bead. She then showed me the 48th bead. I could see that she had looked at the grouping of beads and thought there were 5 in each group, not 10. I told her she had shown me 48. She looked at the string again, "Oh, you mean there aren't 5 beads in each color?" This may display an inability to subitize but also, perhaps, to estimate.

Estimating, even with small quantities, is very difficult for a dyscalculic learner. If a dyscalculic makes a calculation error, their answer may be extremely inaccurate but they will not recognize how far they are from the correct answer because of their inability to estimate. One person in a Facebook group shared that she tipped a restaurant server more than the cost of the meal because she did not have a general idea of how much 15% would be. She had miscalculated with her calculator and multiplied 150% of the bill. In this situation, a dyscalculic would not notice that it would be inaccurate for a $10 meal to have a $15 tip. Another person shared that they had no idea how much a new car should cost, whether it was hundreds or thousands of dollars. My daughter frequently recalls how, in school, she was always off in her guesses of the quantities that the teacher would have in the estimation jars. She told me how she would try her best to study the jars carefully but would always arrive at a guess that was significantly different than those of the rest of the class.

As I prepped dinner one evening, I asked my daughter how many chicken nuggets she would like. She had no idea. I was perplexed and wondered why this simple question was confusing to her. Didn't she know how hungry she was? When she came into the kitchen, she asked if I could pour some nuggets onto the baking sheet so she could show me how many she would like. Suddenly, I realized it was not a matter of her not knowing how hungry she was but that she could not envision that the pile of chicken nuggets she wanted to eat totaled about 6–8.

Those with dyscalculia have a noticeable memory weakness and inability to reliably remember anything related to numbers such as number sequences, calculation steps, and math facts. This will show up in flashcard work when memorizing number facts for subtraction and addition or, especially, with multiplication facts. They will struggle when asked to complete multiple calculation steps in a word problem, and when they are reminded of the steps, they will likely lose track of which step they are on as they work through the problem. It will be hard to remember a sequence of numbers for a pin, phone, or social security number. It is also true that the memory impact seems to come and go. One day, they will accurately recall number sequences or steps in a problem, and the very next day, it will be as if they never learned them and have to start all over again.

One number bond my daughter seemed to get right away by using a dot pattern method was $4 + 5 = 9$. Then, one day, we were playing dice and she puzzled over the 4 and 5 dice patterns, completely unable to remember what the sum was. This happens often. Before I realized it was because of dyscalculia and a low working memory for numbers, we would both become frustrated with her inability to remember the math facts being learned. When she later received her evaluation report from an educational psychologist, it revealed that her working memory for numbers was very low, while her general working memory for anything else was average. Many cultures emphasize the importance of obtaining an instant recall of number facts or "fact fluency," but this skill is something that is almost impossible for dyscalculics to master.

Many dyscalculics display confusion over directions such as left and right or north and south. It is not unusual to have some directional confusion, but dyscalculics display more puzzlement than the average person. Not only are left and right confusing, but dyscalculics may not have a sense of where they are in a space.

On a recent trip to the park, as we were gathering our things to head home, my now 13-year-old daughter ran out of the park gate and off in a direction completely different from where we had parked the car. After looking at each of the parked cars and not seeing ours, she turned back to me and noticed I was watching her. I pointed in the opposite direction, to where we had parked in another parking lot on the other side of the playground. She trotted up to me looking a bit bewildered by her mistake, "Do you think I had no idea because of my dyscalculia?" My honest answer was, "I don't know, but it could be." While more research is needed to learn why this is, it is apparent that lack of directional sense often accompanies dyscalculia.

As mentioned earlier, confusion over money is also a complicated reality for dyscalculics. Our daughter has always struggled to understand the value of coins and notes. I remember a moment when she wanted to buy a gift for a friend. She pulled out a wad of bills and a handful of coins from her purse and piled them in front of me. She had no idea how to figure out how much money she had, how much the item cost, or whether she had anywhere near enough to make the purchase. Another time, she told me how a friend of hers and her friend's little sister liked to play a game where players guess the cost of items on Amazon. My daughter recalled how terrible she was at the game, having no sense of the numbers and the amounts they represented. Many dyscalculics are so overwhelmed by working with numbers that they never apply to jobs for fear that they will not be able to do the basic required tasks related to money. Others are highly anxious over shopping trips and calculating how much they can spend. Working with money requires an understanding of numbers—a knowledge of what they represent, which coins and bills are worth a certain amount, and how to use various calculation methods. All of these are extremely difficult for a dyscalculic.

Not being able to easily recognize number patterns is another sign of dyscalculia. A friend who teaches Montessori preschool shared with me how her students work with a 1–100 numbers chart, working to place all the tiles in the correct locations. Thinking this was a great idea (before I knew about my daughter's dyscalculia), I bought my daughter a nice wood version with tiles numbered 1–100. She never wanted to play with it. Now I know why. To a dyscalculic learner, facing a pile of numbered tiles and a grid to place them on is like being confronted with a plate of mushy vegetables—not fun but supposedly good for you. Later, after we discovered her dyscalculia, she was able to slowly put the numbers together on the board, but I could tell that she struggled to see the number pattern the chart created. It was like she was working with each individual number, trying to find the next one in the sequence and using counting up in ones as her primary method to do so.

Recognizing patterns other than digits is not necessarily complicated. When my daughter works with Cuisenaire Rods (colored rods that represent numbers 1–10, with each rod being a different size and color to correspond to a number), she can easily see the patterns represented. I remember when she first lined up the numbers 1–20 with Cuisenaire Rods, she exclaimed, "Wow, there is a 10 (shown by an orange bar) in each of the numbers 11 through 20!" She was excited to see this pattern that gave an entirely new understanding to what the numbers 11–20 represented.

Difficulty telling time, especially on an analog clock, as well as difficulty understanding time calculations, is another sign of dyscalculia. To understand time, one must not only learn how to read a clock but must also be able to perform quick mental math to determine what part of the hour it is and to calculate differences in times. A common situation you will find in our home is that of our daughter staring at a clock. "Wait," she will say, determined to figure out what time it is on her own. She will stare at it for a bit before turning to announce the time, only to learn that she is incorrect with either the hour or minutes. There also seems to be a lack of sense of time gone by or when something will happen during the day. My daughter will often become anxious about how much time she has to finish an art project because she does not have a sense of where she is in the day. Even if she can correctly determine that it is 3:00 p.m., she has no idea how much time that means she has until bedtime.

Perhaps the most prominent indicator of dyscalculia is a general feeling of anxiety concerning most anything involving numbers. Dyscalculic learners will exhibit anxious behaviors in the classroom and at home when completing math exercises. Because math anxiety is a common experience with various causes, it is not always an indication of dyscalculia. On the other hand, it may be impossible to find a dyscalculic student who does not experience a great deal of anxiety over numbers. The many obstacles they face to grasp basic mathematical concepts, plus the lack of dyscalculia awareness and support, naturally lead to increased anxiety.

chapter 2

Seeking Help

While I became more familiar with the signs of dyscalculia, I observed the many ways this learning disability impacted my daughter in school and at home. I was curious and wanted to better understand this unique difference in how she experienced numbers, so I began reading everything I could find on the subject. Unfortunately, there wasn't much available. A thorough search of our local public library system at that time revealed only two books. Most of what I learned came from searching online and from books I purchased and read.

I quickly became aware of how little I knew about learning disabilities in general and recognized some of the inaccurate assumptions I held about them. One such assumption was that if someone had a learning disability, then they must have lower intelligence. Another was that only a very small percentage of students are learning disabled, which is why the special education classes at school always seem so small.

While I am embarrassed to admit my initial ignorance about what it means to have a learning disability, I share these inaccurate assumptions because I suspect they are common. Incorrect assumptions, such as these, impacted my ability to adequately assess my daughter's situation. My daughter seemed bright, even a bit preco-cious, so the possibility of a learning disability, or what I imagined to be "low intelligence," was not plausible to me. She was articulate from an early age and would often surprise her dad and me with her deep thoughts. She loved to explore, read, and create, with an energy that was never-ending. As a young child and all through her growing up years, she would come alive at night, drawing a magical new world or writing a fantastic story. When she started school, her teachers reported what a great student she was, engaged and excited to learn. All this did not match my idea of someone who might be learning disabled.

Most learning disabilities are a matter of how a person's brain is wired and not an indication of intelligence. In fact, most students with learning disabilities have average or above-average intelligence. I was also surprised to learn that learning and cognitive disabilities impact about one in every five students, which was a much higher percentage of students impacted than I imagined.

My assumptions about learning disabilities would need to be faced and examined because I was pretty sure my daughter had dyscalculia and I had no idea what to do about it. I needed help.

Looking to the School for Help

It was during this time, shortly after first learning about dyscalculia, that I contacted the school to set up a meeting with my daughter's student study team (SST). I wanted to tell them about my suspicion of dyscalculia and ask for their help. This team had already been established for my daughter in the second grade as a beginning inter-vention to address her math difficulties. The team consisted of her teacher, the math specialist, the school counselor, the school psycholo-gist, and me.

During the meeting, I shared the information I had found about dyscalculia. I asked the team if they had heard of this learning disability and if they thought the description matched my daughter's difficulties. I remember struggling to pronounce "dis-cal-CUE-lee-a" and feeling insecure that I had not pronounced it correctly, even though that is how it was pronounced in the online dictionary. My uncertainty was compounded when the school counselor pronounced it as "dis-CAL-cue-lah."

The team offered their observations of my daughter, but no one directly answered my question about whether it could be dyscalculia. They seemed careful and tentative about how they responded to my question, which was confusing to me. The math specialist shared that my daughter was a motivated and focused student, yet she was not progressing as was typical for a student receiving this type of consistent learning support. My daughter's teacher contributed by telling us that my daughter was an engaged and diligent student, but she seemed to be working 10 times as hard on the math lessons as the rest of the class and was still not grasping the material. The school counselor had heard of dyscalculia, but her concluding response was simply, "Let's set up a meeting in the fall with her new fourth-grade teacher and see how things are going at that point."

I was disappointed. I had expected the team to say something more along the lines of, "Yes, it seems very possible that your daughter could have dyscalculia. Let's find out if that is the case." But I also felt overwhelmed and unsure about the official process for identifying and helping students with learning disabilities. I assumed the school would know best, and with no alternative ideas, I agreed to waiting until the following school year to check in and see how my daughter's math was progressing.

Meanwhile, I began to search for information on how to navigate the public school system for help with learning disabilities. It seemed like a complicated and confusing process. One question that arose for me was, "Why had the school not suggested that my daughter be evaluated for dyscalculia?" I had assumed that the school would be the first to notice a possible learning disability and that their job would be to notify parents of any concerns or issues with the student's learning. In our case, I had informed the school that I suspected a learning disability, but they still did not suggest that we have my daughter evaluated to find out if my suspicions were valid. That was perplexing.

I later learned that school district employees (including teachers) were not allowed to suggest to parents that a child be evaluated for a learning disability. It seemed the school district did not want the responsibility that could come with recommending an evaluation. If a teacher were to suggest that there was a possible need for a child to be evaluated, then the school district would be required by law, per the Individuals with Disabilities Education Act (IDEA), to provide the evaluation and adequate learning support if the evaluation confirmed a need. This all would cost the school time and money. If a parent agreed to the teacher's suggestion that a child be evaluated, but then the school district did not conduct an evaluation and provide learning support, the school district could face a lawsuit. By suppressing the number of learning disability evaluations, the school could avoid the extra costs of providing assessment and teaching services to this population, as well as limit the risk of costly lawsuits.

This policy of silence leaves teachers and school specialists in a difficult position. Although they often are the first to see a student's struggles, they are not allowed to suggest to a parent that there may be a learning disability impacting the student or to suggest that the child may benefit from an evaluation. This is why, in our SST meeting, none of the school staff could suggest to me, "Maybe it would be a good idea to evaluate your daughter for a math learning disability."

Help from Fellow Parents

This was a particularly lonely and bewildering time. At several points during my online research sessions, I found myself typing in phrases such as "mom blog on dyscalculia" or "parent support for child with dyscalculia." I found nothing of this personal type of support and wondered what other parents were doing to help their children with dyscalculia. I wished I could talk to someone who would understand what I was going through and point me in the right direction. Surely, I could not be the only parent who was at a loss on how to help their dyscalculic child?

Slowly, I began seeking help, asking my friends if they knew any parents who had children with learning disabilities who could perhaps assist me, and I was given a few names. I remember texting one of the moms whom I did not know: "Hi. We are pretty sure our daughter has dyscalculia. I am having trouble knowing what she needs, determining how to get her help, and navigating the public school. Would you be willing to have a phone conversation sometime and share any thoughts or experience you have that might give me some direction?"

Her gracious reply came immediately: "Sure! Call anytime. Happy to help."

While none of these parent connections knew much about dyscalculia, they knew about learning disabilities and where to go for help. It was from one of these parents that I learned about our rights under the IDEA. In reading through sections of this document and in talking with this parent, I quickly saw that the school's plan of "wait and see" was woefully inadequate. Waiting another seven months would only cause my daughter to fall further behind in math and would not bring us any closer to receiving the help she needed.

Another parent informed me that I could formally request that the school evaluate my daughter for a specific learning disability. The school district may deny my request, but hopefully, with the right language, the right communication, and the right steps, they would approve my request and evaluate my daughter.

I learned from yet another parent that I should request a "comprehensive" evaluation. This parent shared how their own child's learning disabilities were impacted by various physical and cognitive challenges. It was important that my daughter receive a full evaluation to not only look at her math abilities but also executive functions such as memory, cognitive flexibility, attention, and focus. Physical exceptions to the norm should be evaluated as well, such as those related to fine motor skills, large motor skills, sight, and hearing. Later, when the new school psychologist balked at my request for a comprehensive evaluation, this same parent encouraged me to reach out to the school district's learning disability advocate who was able to speak with the psychologist and assured us that we would receive the comprehensive evaluation that we had requested.

Several parents suggested that we also pursue a private (independent) evaluation performed by an educational psychologist outside of the school system. These parents told us that this may be the most helpful step we take in the entire process. Through this type of evaluation, we would learn more about our daughter's specific situation, receive an official diagnosis, and attain critical data we could use for years to come.

The School Evaluation Process

By now, it was June and summer vacation would start within a week. Even with the short timeline, I sent an email to the school principal and psychologist requesting that my daughter be evaluated for dyscalculia at the beginning of the following school year.

I received no response. I sent a follow-up email in September at the start of school, again requesting an evaluation. This time, I received a response, and we began the long process of moving toward a school evaluation while I simultaneously looked into an independent one.

That fall, it felt as if I were working a full-time job to set up both the school and independent evaluations, making sure I jumped through all the hoops correctly. It was exhausting. I was anxious and despaired about how long the process was taking. Meanwhile, our daughter was floundering in math class, seemingly stuck in place while watching her peers move forward in their math skills. While waiting for our daughter to be evaluated, we established a temporary 504 Plan, which gave her a few accommodations in school, such as a calculator, fact charts, and more time on tests. While the accommodations eased some stress in math class, they did not address the real learning challenges—they were a sort of Band-Aid for a larger issue.

For the independent evaluation, I found that all of the recommended educational psychologists had waitlists of 9–12 months. It would be difficult to wait so long, but I found one who was highly recommended by other parents and who accepted our health insurance. I booked my daughter's evaluation appointments for the soonest available, in June at the end of fourth grade.

As we moved through the public school's evaluation process, we experienced pushback from some school personnel. I mentioned previously how the psychologist did not see the need for a comprehensive evaluation and how we had to get the school district's learning disability advocate involved to help us get what was required. Then, there was the physical therapist who became irritated with me for requesting that the evaluation address concerns we had about some of our daughter's large motor skills. At the initial meeting, when I requested the comprehensive evaluation, she declared abruptly, "I work with kids who can't walk. Your daughter is fine."

In contrast to the unhelpful personalities, the math specialist and fourth-grade teacher were present and supportive. One fall weekend, the math specialist invited me to attend a math workshop with her at a local private school that specializes in learning disabilities. She also continued to encourage me by answering the many questions I had during the evaluation and education plan process. My daughter's teacher was also supportive and accommodating, giving my daughter more time to complete assignments and decreasing the amount of math work required. Finally, in November, the school evaluations were scheduled.

It was news to me that the public school's evaluation would not provide a learning disability diagnosis. The school's assessment would simply determine if a student qualified to receive learning support and an individual education plan (IEP). This is one of the reasons we also pursued an independent evaluation—we wanted to receive a professional diagnosis for dyscalculia.

In public school evaluations, there is not one assessment that determines whether a student qualifies for school support in math. Instead, a variety of math assessments are implemented along with general cognitive tests. The math assessments evaluate areas such as math problem-solving, numerical operations, addition-subtraction-multiplication fluency, and computation.

In our situation, the school used the Kaufman Assessment Battery for Children (KABC-II) using the Cattell–Horn–Carroll model for scoring of general cognitive skills and abilities such as problem-solving, reasoning, short- and long-term memory, and visual processing. For math, two tests were implemented: the Wechsler Individual Achievement Test (WIAT-III), for math problem-solving, numerical operations, and numerical fact fluency, and the Kaufman Test of Educational Achievement, Third Edition (KTEA-3), which measures math concepts and applications as well as math computation.

In the United States, there are a couple of ways a student with a learning disability can qualify for special education services in a school evaluation process. One is by demonstrating a need through

Response to Intervention (RTI) and the other is by the discrepancy model. RTI is an examination of how the student has responded to implemented interventions over time in the school setting. An example of one type of intervention would be the two years of small group help my daughter received with the school math specialist. If a child does not respond favorably to the learning support and interventions, they may qualify for support because of their lack of response to the intervention, hence the RTI method.

The second way to qualify for assistance is by the discrepancy model. A student may qualify through this model when there is a severe discrepancy between the student's cognitive abilities and how they perform in a specific area. For our daughter, there was a severe discrepancy between her scores for cognitive ability and how she performed on the math assessments. This substantial discrepancy ended up being what qualified her to receive special education instruction.

After the school evaluation was complete, the school psychologist informed us that our daughter did indeed qualify for special education services and that an IEP would be established for her. She would begin receiving learning support through her IEP in January.

The process of obtaining the school evaluation and resulting IEP took half of the school year to complete, and I was relieved when it was over. Even though we were now halfway through fourth grade, I was hopeful that my daughter would begin receiving the help she needed through special education.

Special Education Obstacles

However, all did not go as smoothly as I had hoped. We immediately faced several obstacles in the implementation of her IEP at school.

The first was that our special education teacher was not trained in or familiar with dyscalculia. She was honest and let us know that she was just now learning about dyscalculia from us. It was extremely disappointing to find out that not even teachers trained in special education knew about this learning disability. Yet, she was warm, caring, flexible, and excited to learn about dyscalculia, and our daughter connected easily with her fun personality, so we felt that was promising and that she was someone we could work with.

The second obstacle was that the school did not have any curriculum that was dyscalculia specific, which meant that our first task was to find a curriculum to use in the classroom and at home. The special education teacher and I searched all over for something to use. The only dyscalculia-specific resource I could find at the time was Ronit Bird's book *The Dyscalculia Toolkit*, which I purchased and gave to the teacher along with some material from Bird's website. We were piecing her math education together with the activities in the book, but we lacked a sequential and trackable learning plan.

The third obstacle was the learning environment in the special education classes. Initially, my daughter was excited that she would have a special class to help her with math. Then, I told her who else would be in her class and her face fell. "What's wrong?" I asked. She told me that those kids were "unexpected" kids. The school used the term unexpected to describe students who demonstrated a behavior that was outside of what was normally expected, such as acting out in disruptive ways or having trouble engaging in socially acceptable ways. My daughter was scared that others would see her as a bad student if she was with those who regularly were unexpected. Also, the disruptive behavior in the classroom was unsettling and distracting to her, which impacted her learning. I brought these concerns up to the special education teacher, and she was able to make a schedule adjustment so that my daughter was placed in another smaller group with less students possessing behavioral issues. However, it meant she had less math instruction per week.

The lack of time my daughter had in special education was an additional frustrating obstacle. The single teacher was maxed out, so our daughter could only receive two, occasionally three, 25-minute sessions per week, and these were shared with other students. It felt like the first several months of special education were simply setting up class expectations and building a relationship with the teacher, but not much progress was made in math for the rest of fourth grade.

Looking back, I sometimes wonder if the school evaluation was worth pursuing. Even after all the hard work to get our daughter evaluated so we could qualify for help, the learning support that was available was not what our daughter really needed. If I were to do it again, perhaps I would have asked more questions about what types of learning support would be provided if she did qualify. Then, I would have decided if it was worth the trouble of having her evaluated.

Positive Growth

One positive change I did notice that year was in my daughter's internal world. Having new language to understand and verbalize her math struggles lessened her anxiety substantially. She was beginning to be curious and notice when her dyscalculia would impact various aspects of her life, and she would say, "Oh, there's that dyscalculia popping up again." She was also developing an ability to advocate for herself in the classroom when she needed help.

In the beginning, she did not want any of her peers to know about her dyscalculia. But, as the year continued, she ended up confiding in three close friends, who responded with kindness, acceptance, and support. She began to talk more openly at home about her dyscalculia as well. As parents, we were intentional about allowing her to express the mix of emotions she had about her learning disability—sometimes anger or sadness and sometimes pride at being unique in this way. One day she exclaimed, "I know why I have a hard time with math. It's because the creative-imaginative-artistic side of my brain is so huge it's pushed out all the math part of my brain. There just isn't as much room for it because the other area is so big!" Her growing self-awareness was helping her see and accept both her struggles and her strengths.

Early that summer, we began another evaluation process, this time with an independent educational psychologist. This evaluation would be helpful in understanding our daughter even further and with gathering a few more tools to use in our journey with dyscalculia.

chapter 3

Another Discovery

By now, it was the beginning of June and fourth grade was coming to an end. In the midst of end-of-year school celebrations and planning for summer vacation, it was also time for the independent evaluation we had scheduled nine months prior.

Our initial appointment was a diagnostic interview, a one-hour appointment for my husband and me to discuss our daughter's situation with the educational psychologist. I felt anxious and weepy as we talked with the psychologist about our daughter's challenges in school, our dyscalculia suspicion, and our difficulty finding help.

I have experienced a similar anxiety before, where I need help but feel on my own and helpless about being able to fix something. I feel it when we take our daughter to her cardiologist appointments every couple of years—to check on her heart post her infant heart surgery. It also comes up whenever she has a round of uncomfortable skin tests and blood draws for her severe food allergies. I experienced this same feeling when my other daughter, our youngest, was in utero and then in the neonatal intensive care unit for three weeks. It is a feeling that I want to protect and provide for my child with the ferocity of a mother bear but also need help because the situation is beyond my capacity to handle alone.

There is also something terrifying about taking a deeper look at a child's struggles and examining them under a microscope. Doing this with a complete stranger can make you feel especially vulnerable. What else would the psychologist uncover? Would it be something more serious than we had anticipated? I felt as if I was also being examined for any faults as a parent and in how I had handled her math struggles so far.

The psychologist was warm, kind, and calm. She was interested in our story and seemed confident she could evaluate our daughter and help us find the resources we needed.

The Evaluation Process

My daughter and I returned to the psychologist's office a week later to begin the first of three appointments for testing. Each time I left my daughter in the psychologist's office, I felt that same nervous anxiety. The three sessions were on different days over a period of a couple weeks and lasted about two hours each time. It was exhausting for both of us. During the evaluations, I waited anxiously in a coffee shop across the street, attempting unsuccessfully to focus on work. After each session, my daughter was famished and completely worn out.

The psychologist first reviewed the test results and records from the school, before administering the following assessments: Wechsler Intelligence Scale for Children (WISC-V), Conners (Conners 3), Behavior Rating Inventory of Executive Function (BRIEF-2), Key Math (KeyMath-3), Wechsler Individual Achievement Test for math fluency only (WIAT-III), Beery-Buktenica Developmental Test of Visual-Motor Integration (Beery), Process Assessment of the Learner for handwriting only (PAL-II), and Behavioral Assessment System for Children (BASC-2). She also included feedback forms from three teachers, individual ones from my husband and me, and a self-feedback worksheet from our daughter.

Discovery of Twice Exceptionality

After the three assessment appointments, my husband and I returned to the psychologist's office for a parent feedback session, excited and nervous to learn what she had found. The psychologist first confirmed our suspicions with a diagnosis of moderate Dyscalculia/Specific Learning Disorder with Impairment in Mathematics. The test results showed a discrepancy with our daughter's high intelligence and cognitive scoring and her lower-than-average math abilities.

The psychologist also shared a new discovery with us. Our daughter was not only learning disabled in math, but she was also considered gifted because of her above-average performance in other areas. Her verbal comprehension and fluid reasoning skills were shown as remarkable, and her visual-spatial reasoning and processing speeds were higher than average. While most of her math performance was low, as low as the 5th percentile of the national average of same-grade peers, her geometry understanding was in the 95th percentile. In the written report, the psychologist wrote that our daughter "may be best understood as a student who is twice exceptional; this means that she has exceptional higher-level cognitive abilities and a mathematics disability."

I had briefly come across the term "twice exceptional" or "2e" in my dyscalculia research online. The term describes students who are identified as gifted (typically two or more standard deviations above the norm) but who perform lower than average in one or more areas because of a learning disability or neurodevelopmental difference. Students who are 2e often have learning disabilities that go undetected because they are able to use their giftedness to hide or compensate for any learning struggles. On the flip side, 2e students may have unnoticed areas of giftedness that are masked by the learning disability. Both of these were true for our 2e child. Her critical reasoning skills would help her solve math problems, and she would often obtain the correct answer, even though she took much longer than the other students and often used unconventional and time-intensive methods because of her low ability to do basic calculations. Because she was performing well in other areas, such as reading and writing, her struggles in math tended to be viewed as not too serious. The areas in which she excelled were also not as noticeable because in assessments, such as standardized tests, she received only an average score. Her high scores in language arts were evened out by her very low scores in math, often giving her an overall average score.

Discovering our daughter's twice exceptionality was transformational. As the psychologist's report indicated, it would be critical that we not only found educational settings that could support her learning disability but also those that would support her areas of giftedness. "She requires educational environments that will challenge and extend her higher-level thinking skills while also providing accommodations and specially designed instruction in mathematics." We needed to support both sides of her unique spectrum and also use the areas she excelled in to support her areas of difficulty.

I share more in Chapter 6 regarding how we tailored her math education to fit her strengths, but in short, we have been able to use her problem-solving and visual-spatial skills to help her understand math in creative ways, as well as use her love for stories and her vivid imagination to connect difficult math concepts.

Included with the full evaluation report was a summary with "Recommendations for School" and "Recommendations for Home," both providing helpful ideas of how to best support our daughter's continued educational and personal growth. We also received a list of private schools in the area that might be a good fit for our daughter as she entered middle school.

The final session in the independent evaluation was a child feedback session in which the psychologist discussed the evaluation findings with my daughter. Together, they created a flyer that featured some of my daughter's strengths, or "Razzle Dazzles" as they called them; a section on how she learned best; a list of helpful tools for math class; specific math challenges to be aware of; and, finally, careers that might be a good fit for her. My daughter was excited to show me the flyer they had created. It was evident that this small exercise was empowering for her. As I looked it over, I noticed "engineer" on the list of possible careers. My daughter was that kid who was always creating, often designing movable contraptions to play with and taking items apart to see how they worked. However, a limiting belief had been planted in my mind by others who made comments such as "Well, I guess she won't want to be an engineer if she has a math learning disability" or "Looks like she'll just have to stay away from jobs involving numbers." The psychologist's affirmation of my daughter's skills reminded me that there are many ways to become a great engineer, or architect, or any number of specific careers. Having a math learning disability did not need to be limiting.

My husband and I ended the evaluation process feeling encouraged. We better understood our daughter's individual strengths and challenges and were better equipped to find an educational situation that would fit what she needed to be successful in school. Later that year, we were also able to use the evaluation scores and findings as we looked into middle school possibilities. Overall, the independent educational evaluation did end up being one of the most helpful steps in our dyscalculia journey, just as the supportive parents suggested it would be.

Practical and Financial Obstacles

Having gone through the process of an independent educational evaluation, I can say without a doubt that it was worth the effort, time, and money. However, I know that many parents may have reservations or questions about going through such an evaluation.

When a child is struggling in school, parents sometimes say things such as "I'm sure getting a new teacher next year will make a difference" or "We are going to try a new way of eating … tutoring … a new parenting plan … first to see if that will help." I imagine that these parents are hoping that their child's struggles are nothing as complicated as a learning disability or neurological difference and that they can be managed by a simpler solution than a psychological evaluation. It may also be a sign that they are hesitant or have deeper reservations about having their child evaluated.

There are many reasons parents may resist having their child evaluated. Some of these objections are practical; others are internal and maybe even unknown. A few of these possible obstacles could be the amount of time and energy required, the financial cost, or unconscious fears.

One obvious and practical obstacle is the sheer overwhelming feeling regarding the long arduous process involved in having a child evaluated. There is much work to do and so many questions that need to be answered. How do we find the right professional? Will health insurance cover the evaluation? How do we fit the appointments into our schedule? Is the help local or do we need to travel? How long is the waitlist? The entire process is a great deal of work. With so many parents already busy and overwhelmed, it is no wonder that many feel they cannot take on one more thing.

While pursuing evaluation is a sizable task, in the end, it can lighten the parents' workload and their anxiety, providing a smoother and clearer direction forward. It is worth the initial hard work to know more about what your child's unique situation is so you can make the best choices specific to what they need. It can actually save time and headaches later because you have a better sense of what to do. While I hear parents say they wish they had their child evaluated sooner, I have not yet heard one share that a solid evaluation was not worth it.

As we were looking into the evaluation, I learned a few helpful tips about how to choose an evaluator. It is important to investigate whether the educational psychologist is fully licensed in the state in which they practice; you want to retain the services of a qualified and experienced professional. It is also critical to ask if, and to what degree, they are familiar with dyscalculia specifically. Not all evaluators are. While a long waitlist can be frustrating, it can also be a good sign that an evaluator is highly sought after. The fact that your insurance covers them does not ensure that the evaluator is experienced or excels in their field. The best way to determine the quality of the evaluator is to read recommendations from several other sources. One great place to find good evaluators is through online or in-person parent support groups. Parents are usually happy to share their experiences, whether good or bad, with other parents asking for help. You may also ask health professionals you trust if they know of any qualified neuropsychologists or educational psychologists they would recommend. Another great way to get a feel for an evaluator and learn more about their experience and expertise is through a short "meet and greet" appointment, which most professionals offer for free. It is worth the time to make the best choice possible regarding who evaluates your child.

Financial cost is another legitimate concern and can be a huge obstacle when it comes to independent evaluations. When I heard that a private evaluation was going to cost between $4,000 and $6,000, I was unsure how our family could make it happen. Some parents may hear the cost and immediately decide that an evaluation is unaffordable. Sometimes, it is just not an option; other times, though, there are ways around the cost obstacle.

When we were researching how we could have our daughter evaluated, we were living on a tight budget in a large city with a high cost of living. I wondered how we would afford it, but I booked the appointments anyway before I figured out how we would pay for them. I knew I had nine months to plan and save.

To start, I looked into our healthcare coverage. Because we were self-employed, we did not have employer-provided health insurance but instead purchased a health plan for our family each year. It turned out that the educational psychologist was in network with our insurance plan and that it might be possible to have the evaluation covered by our health insurance. I needed to figure out just how much it would cost us to do this.

I called the office of the psychologist with whom we had booked our appointments and spoke with the bookkeeper, who was happy to help me with any information I needed in regard to working with the health insurance company. I asked for the insurance billing codes (CPT codes) that would be used for all the visits and tests. I also asked for the estimated quantity of each billing code that would be used. A provider may use 8–10 test units, so one billing code would be billed for each individual test. I also asked for the billed amount of each of these items. This is the cost that the evaluator would bill the insurance company. Usually, the actual amount we would pay would be lower than the billed amount because health insurance companies put a cap on how much they will pay providers for services.

After I compiled a list of all the billing codes, I called our health insurance company to ask about the coverage on each one. I did not tell them I was asking for coverage about a learning disability; I did not want them to view this as an "educational" inquiry and not health related. I simply asked about each billing code I had been given. The representative went through each billing/CPT code and told me for each one whether it was an item they would cover, if the item required my deductible to be met first, and the percentage they would cover. I made detailed notes of all this information, including the name of the person I talked with and the date of our conversation. Some of the items required that we meet our deductible first, while others were partially paid by insurance before meeting the deductible. The insurance company also informed me as to where each item fit in my benefit plan. The tests fit under "Diagnostic Testing and Labs" and the visits with the psychologist fit under either a "Specialist Visit" or "Mental Health."

During the insurance company call, I also asked if the psychologist visits or diagnostic labs would require a referral from our pediatrician or a preauthorization from the insurance company. Some insurance companies require a referral from a preferred provider or a preauthorization before they will cover the cost. A referral is not simply your doctor recommending a psychologist. It is a process where your doctor sends a formal referral to the psychologist you want to see and the latter completes the required insurance paperwork with the insurance company prior to your visit. If a preauthorization is required, the psychologist will need to fill out preauthorization paperwork and receive approval from the health insurance company before your child is seen. In our situation, for our specific plan at the time, neither was required.

When I say that the evaluation was "covered" by insurance, I do not mean that they paid all the costs but simply that it was a benefit listed on our health insurance plan and the company agreed to partially pay for the appointments and tests.

From this information, I was able to have a closer estimate of the total cost for our family. It took some time to figure out how much of our deductible we had met so far, which appointments and tests would be paid for, and how much each item would cost at most based on the billed amount. It gave us a possible range of $1,000–$2,000, depending on the number of appointments and tests actually completed, and allowed us to move forward with beginning to save the funds that would be due in nine months.

Some may wonder if it is worth having a provider bill the insurance company if the deductible is so high that you are unlikely to reach it. I believe it is. Sometimes, the insurance company gives a lower allowable amount that a provider can bill, which lowers the amount you pay. For example, the provider cost may be $200, but the allowable amount is $120, so that is what you pay, saving you a bit of money. Also, it takes some planning, but you may consider taking care of any other medical issues your family may have in the same calendar year so you can meet your deductible more easily and maybe even reach your out-of-pocket maximum, which is the point at which the insurance company pays 100% of your medical bills.

Many individuals fear that working through the insurance company is too difficult, but if finances are a hindrance to an independent evaluation, I believe it is worth the time and energy to see if you can first get help through your health insurance company. Most providers are happy to help you work through any insurance processes. In our case, the final cost ended up being about $1,500 instead of about $4,500. That price reduction was definitely worth all the calls and hours spent pouring over figures.

There are situations in which a family's health insurance will not cover any of the costs, or a family simply does not have health insurance. When this is the case, there are a few other options worth researching.

First, some universities offer reduced cost evaluations as part of their training program. You can usually find information on this in their psychology or education department. Even if the website of your local university does not mention anything about a sliding scale or reduced cost, call and ask about the option anyway. The waitlists for these free or reduced cost services can be long, but they are long anyway for a good private evaluator. One thing to note is that the evaluators are usually students, so they will not be as experienced. However, this alternative can save you money, and the university may have access to cutting edge research on learning disabilities, which could be a great help.

Second, find an evaluator who offers services at a reduced rate or on a sliding scale based on income. This option is best to ask about after you have met with the professional for a meet and greet appointment and they have heard your story and can see that you are fully invested in the evaluation process. An alternative that has become increasingly available due to the global pandemic of 2020 is the provision of online evaluations at a lower rate. Places such as The Scholars' Grove[1] offer comprehensive evaluations online at an affordable price.

Third, there are some private institutions that provide evaluations at a reduced cost. If you are in the United States, check with your state's local chapter of the Learning Disabilities of America Association for a list of places providing this service. When I contacted our local chapter, they informed me of a couple of programs I was not previously aware of that offered reduced cost evaluations.

Finally, in the United States, if your child has already been evaluated by the public school but you disagree with the evaluation results, the IDEA allows you the right to request an independent evaluation at public expense. However, this option could be slow and frustrating, as it involves participating in a legal hearing and there is no guarantee the hearing will warrant an independent evaluation. To learn more about this option, educate yourself on the laws related to independent educational evaluations in the IDEA, Section 300.502.

It is also important to note that as I gain further understanding of my identity as a white woman living in a wealthier part of the country, I realize that I have much to learn about my own privilege and the resources I have access to and often take for granted. I am cognizant of the fact that having the ability and means to even consider having my child privately evaluated for a learning disability is not a situation equally accessible to every person. I do not have any solutions for this, but it is a serious inequity problem that I want to acknowledge.

Facing Fears and Difficult Emotions

The hesitancies and objections that can be most difficult to detect and work through are the ones that we may not even be aware of. This is where subconscious fears and unwanted emotions impact our choices without us realizing it. Though they are the most difficult to identify, they can be the most powerful influences on our actions and decisions.

Having a child evaluated for a learning disability may bring all kinds of fears to the surface. What will I do if my child *does* have a learning disability? Will I be able to handle the challenges of having a child with such needs?

This reminds me of the *Seinfeld* episode where George has a white spot on his upper lip and he does not want to have it seen by a doctor because he is afraid of what the doctor will find and that it may be cancer. It is ironic because, of course, if it is something as serious as cancer, it will be there regardless of whether he chooses to acknowledge it. We all have areas in our life that are hard to look at because we fear what we will find. While we know deep down that ignorance is not really bliss, sometimes, it feels even scarier to know our reality than it is to continue living in denial.

We may also have unwanted feelings about what others will think if our child has a learning disability. Will they think our child is less intelligent or defective in some way? How will it impact how they view us as parents or how they look at our family?

Looking at our child's struggles may also prompt painful memories and stories from our own past. As we were going through the evaluation process, I remembered that, in middle school, I had to go in after school for extra help in math, while my younger sister was at the same level of math as I was. There were feelings of embarrassment that I, the bigger sister who usually received straight A's, needed extra help, while my little sister did not. Other memories surfaced as well—of being a child who was afraid of failure and who had an intense drive to succeed in school. The process of having my daughter evaluated also triggered feelings of shame and inadequacy, which I then had to spend time processing with my therapist and also with my husband. I have heard stories of parents recalling memories of their own parent yelling at them as they struggled with flashcards or math drills. Others experienced peers ridiculing them for learning challenges.

It is these deeper emotions and memories that can unearth unspoken fears and unexamined limiting beliefs that we have unknowingly held onto. These, in turn, can hinder our ability to assist our child with their own struggles. It helps to work these out with a professional or a trusted friend who can support you. Again, this sometimes hard work will make the rest of the journey much smoother.

chapter 4

The Research

When I first began trying to learn about dyscalculia, I had little success finding scientific research on the subject. I eventually gave up and focused on supporting my daughter emotionally and with her math education. Then, Brian Butterworth published his book *Dyscalculia: From Science to Education*,[1] which I found to be the most comprehensive compilation and helpful resource on the research surrounding dyscalculia. Butterworth is an emeritus professor at the Institute of Cognitive Neuroscience at University College London and has published numerous articles and books on dyscalculia.

These are a few of my original questions about dyscalculia and what I have learned so far, mostly from Butterworth's work.

Who came up with the word dyscalculia and why is it so hard to pronounce?

I have not met anyone who does not stumble over how to say "dyscalculia" the first time they use it. Sometimes, they figure it out, but mostly, they cease trying and avoid using the word entirely. We have Ladislav Kosc to thank for this complicated label. Kosc was a researcher who first used the term dyscalculia in the early 1970s to describe a disorder of mathematical abilities originating in the brain.[2] The name's meaning can be broken down like this:

dys = bad or difficult

cal-cul = having to do with calculating numbers or amounts

-ia = a state or disorder

Basically, the word defines a disorder in which someone is bad at or has difficulty calculating numbers. The best way to learn to pronounce this word is by breaking it down into its five syllables, with the emphasis on the middle syllable: dis-kal-**kyoo**-lee-*uh*. The most common error in pronunciation occurs when people omit the two-syllable "lee-uh" at the end and change it to a one syllable "luh." I have noticed a slight difference between the British and American pronunciations: the British say "cu/kyoo" with more of a "coo" sound, while Americans tend to pronounce the "cu/kyoo" similarly to how they say the letter "Q."

When was dyscalculia first recognized?

While Kosc was the first to coin the term in the 1970s, it did not become more widely recognized until much later. The *Diagnostic and Statistical Manual of Mental Disorders* (the DSM) IV by the American Psychiatric Association was published in 1994 and included the diagnosis of dyscalculia, and in 2001, the United Kingdom's Department for Education and Skills recognized dyscalculia as a condition making it difficult to acquire mathematical skills.[3] Sometimes, researchers or professionals refer to "developmental dyscalculia," which is just a way to separate dyscalculia as something one is born with, which is different than "acquired dyscalculia," which occurs when someone loses mental capacity for math due to trauma such as a brain injury.[4]

What causes dyscalculia?

As he explains the various research, Butterworth presents the case that the dyscalculic mind has a core deficit in the part of the brain responsible for processing numbers.[5] This deficit manifests as a noticeable lack of number sense and abnormality in how the brain's network processes numbers. Some researchers believe it is because the connection between numbers and sets is not well established in the brain.[6] In one study, the region of the brain responsible for numerical processing had lower gray matter density (the cells responsible for activity) in those with dyscalculia.[7] This core deficit is present in about 5% of the population worldwide.[8]

Developmental dyscalculia is something an individual is born with, not something that develops because of a lack of education or training.[9] There has been some research that supports a possible connection between learning disabilities and prebirth trauma, such as preterm birth, low birthweight, and prenatal alcohol syndrome,[10] but not enough for any conclusive findings.

When my daughter first showed signs of struggling in math, I wondered if I had done something wrong or messed up in some way with her education. Did I not do enough to help her learn her numbers at home as a young child? Was it detrimental to her that we could not afford to send her to preschool? It was reassuring to learn that these are not the causes of dyscalculia. While my daughter did not have prebirth trauma, she did have severe trauma immediately after birth when she underwent heart surgery at five days old. Was this trauma something that could cause a delay in the development of the number processing part of her brain? It is a question I am unable to answer.

Is dyscalculia something you outgrow?

There is no evidence that one can outgrow dyscalculia. Dyscalculics who are now adults still struggle daily with numbers and calculations. Most never knew about their disability as a child, were never assessed for the learning disability, and never received learning support to mitigate its impact. There is some practical evidence that with proper educational methods, an understanding of numbers can be developed, but nothing solid has been followed and studied thoroughly. Further research needs to be done to determine if indeed someone can outgrow dyscalculia—if the brain is able to change the wiring in the number processing region.

Why is more not known about dyscalculia?

Often, when I have questions about why something is the way it is, my husband jokingly replies, "I have one word: money." I think this probably is the case with dyscalculia. Research must be funded, and without a society even being aware of the impact that dyscalculia has on 3–8% of its population, funds are not going to be adequately allocated in this area. Universities need funding to conduct costly long-term experiments and research. Schools need funding to provide testing and educational support for dyscalculics. Parents need money to hire independent educational psychologists to perform diagnostic evaluations. If educational or government authorities recognized dyscalculia, then they would need to provide support for those with the condition.[11] This would cost them money. Maybe this is why some estimate that the research on dyscalculia is 30 years behind that of dyslexia.

Who are the dyscalculia experts?

I have been most impressed with the information coming out of the United Kingdom. Most of the books and resources I have found on dyscalculia are from that country, from authors, such as Dorian Yeo, Brian Butterworth, Ronit Bird, Jane Emerson, Patricia Babtie, and Steve Chinn, and centers such as The Emerson House and The Dyscalculia Network. I have discovered that many of the best teachers for dyscalculic students were taught by or followed the methods of Dorian Yeo, a pioneer in the field of dyscalculia.[12] Daniel Ansari is another researcher who is heading up studies on dyscalculia; he received his doctorate from University College London and is now a professor at Canada's Western University and head of the Numerical Cognition Laboratory. Dr. A.M. Schreuder with Dyscalculia Services, United States, is another expert in the field.

There are more questions than answers about dyscalculia. We have a long way to go. And, though we are only just beginning in many ways, there is hope that the research is expanding. More interest and awareness will bring about funding resources, which will help grow a field of investigation still in its infancy.

chapter 5

Transitions

My daughter's fifth-grade year was full of transitions. Our family was in the process of considering a move to a nearby town just outside of the city where my husband and I had lived for over 20 years. Our house was the only home our daughters had known. This alone was a huge transition to consider, and there were others.

Our small elementary school was undergoing renovation, and we were at a satellite location in a nearby neighborhood. In addition to that, three of my daughter's closest friends had enrolled at other schools, leaving only one close friend at school, and she was placed in a different class. It was also the time of year to look into middle school options for the following year. Many of the conversations with my mom friends were about which school tours we had scheduled and the pros and cons of private versus public school. It was a bit overwhelming and seemed like so much fuss over middle school. Yet, with the new discovery of our daughter's giftedness and learning disability, we were not convinced that the public school system was the best place for her.

We began the process of looking into and touring some of the private schools the educational psychologist had recommended. Most of them were small and so we hoped our daughter could receive personalized support for her learning disability while being challenged and encouraged in her areas of giftedness. We knew that a private school education was out of our means financially, but we decided that we could apply for financial aid and see what happened. In addition to researching options in the city, we also looked into options in the small town we were considering moving to. However, I quickly became discouraged by the fact that even in the private school arena, very few educators, if any, had heard of dyscalculia. Some of the schools were equipped with staff and classes for students with learning challenges, but I did not find any with staff trained to support dyscalculia specifically. The administrators at a couple schools admitted that if she was enrolled, we would have to find support for our daughter's dyscalculia outside of school. It was disheartening to imagine paying the high cost of private tuition and not even have the learning support we needed most.

Meanwhile, my daughter continued fifth grade at the elementary school she had attended since first grade. It felt different from her previous years because of the temporary building and her close friends no longer being in attendance. One part of her schooling that she did enjoy was the time with her special education teacher, whom she saw three times a week. In the short 25-minute sessions, they played math games using hands-on math manipulatives and created a special binder for my daughter full of fun math activities. Her anxiety around math lessened as we continued to talk about her dyscalculia at home and to work closely with her teacher as the latter provided a safe learning environment at school.

My daughter continued in the general education math class but was increasingly unable to keep up or understand the instruction. As part of her IEP, the school provided a teaching assistant in the classroom during math. This initially seemed like a good idea, but the assistant was not familiar with dyscalculia. Her explanations of the material were confusing and frustrating to my daughter, who would avoid receiving help from her at all costs, even telling the assistant, "I think I'm getting it now" (even though she was not). We made a plan with her teacher that if my daughter did not understand the concepts being taught, she could pull out her special education math binder and work on worksheets from there until the teacher could help her. But it was still upsetting and embarrassing when the other students would notice her pulling out her binder because she did not understand the lessons and could not keep up with them. Even when the teacher had a moment to finally help her, she was not able to provide the help my daughter needed because she was not familiar with the nuances of dyscalculia. As the year progressed, my daughter became more upset and anxious in math class. The gap of math comprehension and learning between herself and her classmates only continued to grow larger.

Another difficulty that year was that the fifth-grade class was especially unruly and the teacher spent a great deal of time leading class conversations about expectations and classroom behavior. The noise, the talking during instruction, and the rude interactions between students did not create an environment in which my daughter could even develop the areas she excelled in, such as reading and writing, let alone focus on her learning challenges. She began regularly asking for permission to work on her classwork in the hall or in a quiet corner of the nearby special education room. She was disappointed that the classroom did not provide an environment where she could dive into writing as much as she wanted, and she was often returning home from school frustrated and exhausted. One day she articulated the frustration, "I go to bed and get all rested. Then, I go to school and spend the whole day doing things I don't want to do. Then, I come home, but I'm too tired to do all the things I want to do!"

What was it she *wanted* to do? She wanted to write a book. She wanted to learn the Spanish language and visit a Spanish-speaking country. She wanted to grow her drawing and art skills and become an accomplished artist. She wanted to be outside and explore all the interesting plants, birds, and bugs she saw.

It seemed that the school environment was negatively impacting her innate curiosity and love for learning. So, with only two and a half months until the end of school, we pulled her out of almost all her classes at public school and made the choice to homeschool part time while leaving her enrolled in special education math only. We had already made the choice a couple of months prior to move to the smaller town that following summer, which made the decision to withdraw easier.

Dual Enrollment

I was familiar with our state's laws on "dual enrollment," a provision for students to be enrolled part time in two educational settings, such as in a private and a public school or in home education and public school. After confirming that my daughter could keep her IEP for special education math while also having home-based instruction, I filled out the simple one-page "Declaration of Intent to Provide Home-Based Instruction" document, detailing that my daughter would continue her special education math class and complete the remainder of her instruction at home.

Three times a week, my daughter would sign in at school, attend special education math for the 25-minute class, sign out, and finish her school day at home. For those two and a half months, she worked mostly independently because I was finishing up my part-time job and getting the house ready to sell and my husband was working full time. She began learning Spanish with the Duolingo app, worked with a writing tutor once a week on her short stories, participated in a pottery class with one of her friends, and spent the rest of the time creating art and reading books.

Some parents are surprised to hear that dual enrollment or part-time enrollment is an option. While the laws and requirements around this vary in each state and country, it can be a great option for students requiring greater support than is available in school. One reason this option may not be widely known, even in states where it is allowed, is that most public schools do not want students to be partially enrolled because the school receives less money from the state if a student attends only part time.

I first experienced this dual-enrollment option in my own childhood. My kindergarten through high school education included years in public school, private school, and homeschool. In middle school, I was homeschooled, but I was also enrolled in two advanced placement classes in the public school. This dual enrollment also helped provide a smoother transition from a year of full-time homeschool to full-time public high school.

I was also familiar with this unconventional educational option from my sister. She has four boys and has creatively navigated their education over the years. Most of their education has been in public school, but there have been years where she has partially homeschooled them. One year, she homeschooled the older two while they continued at the public school for specialist classes such as music, physical education, and library. Another year, one of her sons needed more support in particular classes, so she homeschooled him for those classes while he also took a few classes at the public school. After a year of extra attention and focus on those subjects, he returned to full-time public school. Recently, my sister removed one of her younger boys from public school for a year. He was showing signs of giftedness and needed more challenging and stimulating material while also requiring extra help with emotional regulation. He thrived in the combination of the home learning environment mixed with the few classes and social activities he continued at school. It was such a successful year that they have continued for a second year of dual enrollment.

One resource that has been particularly helpful to me in this area of creative school options in multiple school settings is the book *Rethinking School* by Susan Wise Bauer. I highly recommend it for any parent seeking the best learning environment for their child and who is open to outside-the-box thinking on ways to do that.

A New School District

In the process of moving, we enrolled our daughter in the new town's public middle school because it seemed the most promising and most affordable option. I had discovered there was some awareness about twice exceptionality among the staff; one administrator had even heard of dyscalculia and had participated in a training seminar with 2e expert Susan Baum. My daughter's previous IEP was transferred to the new district, and without requiring another evaluation, they established a new IEP for her dyscalculia. We were pleasantly surprised to discover that instead of just three sessions of 25 minutes for special education math instruction, she would now receive five 1-hour sessions per week! She would not attend general math education at all, instead attending a special education math class with a small group of students during math time. The special education teacher told me on the phone that she thought she herself might have a level of dyscalculia, which I took to mean that she would truly understand my daughter's struggles. It all seemed amazing. We were hopeful this would be a great year for her in math.

However, pretty quickly, my daughter began coming home with lengthy and involved math worksheets for homework from special education math. The material did not represent the teaching methods I had come to understand as most effective for dyscalculics.

My daughter, who had been excited about her new math class, was already expressing anxiety and stress about the class. I encouraged her to stick with it, hopeful that surely it would all even out soon.

Yet, instead of diminishing, my concerns continued to grow daily. It was curious to me that there were no hands-on learning materials in the classroom, such as counting beads, Cuisenaire rods, geometric shapes, different types of dice, or number tracks. I asked my daughter about this and she said the students could ask for tools to help but that they had to request them and go to the front of the class to retrieve anything they needed. This was embarrassing enough for middle schoolers, but the situation was made worse because the teacher discouraged use of anything besides pencil and paper. This did not correspond with what I had read was most helpful for students with dyscalculia; they need concrete learning materials with which they can interact.

One day, my daughter came home especially upset. During the day's lesson on decimals, the teacher had written on the board "Larger Numbers . Smaller Numbers" with the decimal in the middle. The students were told to copy this in their notebooks. In her own notebook, my daughter wrote "Whole . Parts" with the decimal in the middle. When the teaching assistant came around to check on students' work, she asked my daughter what she was doing. My daughter explained that decimals made the most sense to her as a whole-to-parts setup. The assistant responded that she needed to erase her work and copy it exactly as it was done on the board. My daughter did as she was told, erased her work and rewrote it, but I am pretty sure she did not learn anything else that day while feeling she had done something wrong by drawing out the decimal system in a way that made the most sense to her.

On a few different days, my daughter was given several math tests. One time, she asked the teacher about this because she knew that her previous IEP provided an accommodation for less math testing. The teacher responded defensively, causing my daughter to feel belittled for inquiring about the tests she was being given.

I noticed my daughter was beginning to bite her nails and display anxious behaviors I had not seen in a while. I asked her if she noticed any other students who seemed nervous in class and how the teacher responded to them. My daughter said if someone seemed nervous and was making busy movements with their hands or body, the teacher would say, "Stop that and listen" or "Stop doing that and focus." Another behavior the teacher did not allow was doodling on the borders of a math worksheet or notebook. This was especially troubling for my daughter because one of the ways she learned best was through drawing pictures of the concept or sketching out a math problem with images. Sometimes, she would draw out pictures to help her sort out or describe the feelings she was having in class. When math was a struggle, she would often do a sketch of a superhero character she had created years prior, Dyscalculia Master. This character could often be seen flying above the math page, reminding my daughter that she could overcome the difficult math work. But this "doodling" was not allowed by the teacher. She wanted clean and tidy notebooks and worksheet pages.

This lack of emotional intelligence and awareness on the part of the teacher was baffling to me. Standard special education teaching skills should involve the ability to help students with anxiety and an understanding that students' anxious behaviors are communicating that they are not doing well and need help.

One day after school, my daughter spent a great deal of time struggling through a full worksheet of math problems. After about an hour, I told her she had done enough and that she should turn it in without finishing. My daughter was afraid to have incomplete work, so I wrote a note at the top of the page to the teacher and explained that I had told my daughter that she had done enough problems for the day and that she needed to have time to recover and rest after school.

The next day, I received a call from the teacher regarding the unfinished worksheet. I explained that there were too many problems on the homework sheets and that my daughter was spending about an hour every day working to solve the few problems she could manage. The teacher agreed to assign less problems to her in the future. While she was on the phone, I brought up a few of my other concerns. I asked about the lack of math manipulatives available in the classroom, the tidy notebook requirement, and the primary use of worksheets for learning. I could sense the same defensiveness my daughter had encountered with the teacher over testing. During our conversation, she said several times, "I can't do that because of the school district standards" or "The school district doesn't allow that." I could see that she was in a hard place, unable to tailor to the needs of struggling students perhaps because of the standards placed on her by the school district. These were most likely standards for the average student, not for students who had learning disabilities and needed differentiated learning. From what the teacher reported, the school district wanted students to use mostly paper and pencil strategies and not calculators or concrete manipulatives. They wanted tidy worksheets and learning by rote or memorization. That is all fine for the average learner but not for students in this classroom struggling because of a math learning disability.

I was frustrated and angry with the class management and felt deeply disappointed that the entire situation was not going at all like we had hoped. My daughter was not receiving the support she needed, and the circumstances were being made worse by the negative impact of the teaching staff. I required help as I was not sure of the best way to communicate our needs to the teacher. So, I called the administrator I had spoken with during enrollment. I explained that my daughter was loving school but having a terrible time in math class. I was surprised at the teaching style and the work being given because it did not match what I knew was best for students who needed differentiated learning, especially those with dyscalculia. I wondered what I should do, especially with a teacher who seemed to become easily defensive. In response, the advocate suggested that I write an email to this teacher and share what I knew about my daughter's learning style and needs, and to copy her on the email. So, I did; I formulated a detailed letter and emailed it to the teacher.

Dear Ms. S:

Thank you for chatting with me on the phone last week. Since then, I have been thinking about how to set up my daughter for success in your classroom. I would love to collaborate with you in finding ways of learning that connect for my daughter in the way she is wired to learn. You have so many students you care for, each with their own individual needs, and it is the difficult job of yours to know how to tailor the learning to each child.

I think one way I can help is by giving you a cheat-sheet view of some things I know about my daughter—what she loves, how she learns, and where she gets stuck in the learning process. I also have some ideas I would like to run by you and see if you think they might work for you as you teach her.

It will take us some time this year to find the best formula for my daughter's successful learning, but I'm up for the journey and want to work with you as a team as we go along. These are some initial thoughts as we approach the beginning of this process.

About her learning style

I think you probably saw this on my daughter's education psychology testing results, but not only does she have dyscalculia, she is a 2e kid. (I'm assuming you are familiar with that term, but if not, I'm very happy to share more about what that means.) Our family is seeking a strengths-based approach to her learning as a student with highly capable abilities as well as a learning disability.

Her strengths and interests

- She loves reading and writing. She is currently reading at the 11th-grade level and is an avid book reader. She is also talented in creating stories; for fun at home, she writes stories and poems.
- She possesses advanced problem-solving abilities, which are a huge asset for her. When given the space to be creative and curious, she is above average at finding solutions to various problems.
- She has a visual-spatial learning style. It may seem odd but she loves geometry and the study of things in physical space. She loves to create and build structures as well as construct and engineer new inventions such as pulleys and other things that work.
- She is deeply curious and a passionate learner.

Her struggles

- number sense
- estimating
- telling and keeping up with time
- understanding and executing arithmetic functions

When it comes to learning, she shuts down in these situations

- Not feeling understood or when there is only one "right" way to do something, especially when that way doesn't make sense to her.
- Classwork or homework on worksheets. She cries in frustration and dread at the sight of a worksheet.

- Boredom when the topic being presented is something she already understands or is a repetition of the same material/problems. (Kids with dyscalculia do not reach the place of automation in arithmetic, so long segments of time in repetition do not have the same helpfulness as they do for a child without dyscalculia.)

- Chaotic or loud places. If a room is loud or full of disruptive kids, she is easily distracted and unable to focus. She can readily feel the anxiety in others, which makes it hard for her to concentrate in emotionally or physically chaotic environments.

- When material doesn't make sense to her and she is unable to grasp a concept, but the material continues to be explained in the same way. This makes her feel stupid and she shuts down.

Ideas to keep the light in her eyes and her passion for learning growing

- Creative problem-solving: She loves to problem solve. If there is a way to present a real problem that she can solve, she will be highly engaged, especially if it revolves around something she is interested in. For example, she is currently interested in flying. There are all sorts of math problems connected to this. And we could let her run with them, giving her guidance on how to set up the math problems connected to this concept. I have other ideas as well.

- Replace worksheets with parent-led games/activities: Instead of doing the worksheets sent home each day, could my daughter commit to spending 20 minutes with me on a game or activity related to the same subject? I recently purchased a curriculum piece for teaching fractions and decimals to kids with dyscalculia that would be a great place to start and would correspond with the worksheets you send home.

- Openness to other ways of understanding: She understands most math concepts differently than how the average person does. And, even though you yourself have some
dyscalculia, she may understand or learn differently than
how you teach these concepts. It would help my daughter
greatly if she could be allowed some space to grasp the
ideas in a way that she is wired to learn, even if her meth-
odology doesn't make sense to others. For example, the
other week, she wrote down a decimal concept in her math
notebook, demonstrating she understood the topic. However, it was different than the way it was drawn on the
board. (She had written "Whole . Parts" instead of "Larger
Numbers . Smaller Numbers.") Your aid told her that her
method was incorrect and made her erase what she had
written and copy the way everyone else was writing it. This
sort of lack of openness to different ways of understanding
was upsetting to my daughter and is the type of behavior
that will only cause her to shut down (not to mention the
impact it may have on other children).

- Creative expression and emotionally aware conversations: We talked about this on the phone. I believe it would
help if the rigidity over drawing in the math notebook
could be lessened for my daughter. However, I think, along
with that, it would benefit both of you to have conversations when this is happening. Another gift of hers is that
she's both very articulate and more emotionally intelligent
than most kids her age; she will often know quite quickly
what she is feeling and be able to verbalize that to an
adult who is understanding and emotionally safe. Ask her
about what she is experiencing in the moment—without
shaming. Is she doodling because she is bored with the
material? Is she doodling because it is helping her process
and understand the material? Is she needing a creative
outlet because she is overloaded with info? On this, I realize that the school has an ideal of "neat work." This is

an interesting priority that I'd be happy to address with the school administration if you receive pushback. I can explain to them how a 2e kid, such as my daughter, learns, especially if that would help free you to ease up on the "neat notebook" requirement.

- Use colorful, hands-on, visual tools: She is very creative and visual; she loves to create and invent things. If math situations can be incorporated into something she is physically creating, she will be more engaged and learn much more quickly. She would benefit greatly from using manipulatives daily. Some really helpful tools are several colorful dice, Cuisenaire rods, a colorful number line with positive and negative numbers, and dot-counting flip cards, among others. These sorts of vibrant tools will help her immensely. On the phone, you mentioned to me that the school wants less hands-on work and more pen and paper. I think this idea stems from a lack of understanding of how children with math learning disabilities learn, and I am happy to also fight this battle for you, by talking with the administration about her particular needs as a 2e kid. I know you want to keep the standards and follow the rules and I respect that. But, if you are willing to try some more interactive learning styles with her, I will work on forging ahead in regard to the school rules.

- Discussion before testing: I would like to have a conversation with you first before my daughter takes any math tests—whether state, or school, or diagnostic tests for you to know where she stands. That way, we can talk about the nature of the test, the method, and the reason for it, before deciding together if the benefits of the test are worth the anxiety it causes her.

Well, my initial list of ideas is quite lengthy. I'm happy to meet in person to chat more about what I've written. And I would love your feedback on some of the suggestions I have for making this a successful class for my daughter.

I realize we have an IEP meeting next week. I'm hoping some of these ideas will help us shape an IEP that is a successful guiding document.

Thank you,
Laura

A New Plan

Our IEP meeting with the new school was a week away. My husband and I continued to talk over the school situation and what we should do about it. We came to the conclusion that even if the school was able to provide some learning tools, and even if they could implement some of my suggestions, the reality was that the special education teacher was clearly not able to provide the type of emotional support and awareness that was needed, especially in her current classroom. It was evident that she was not trained in the most effective ways to teach students with dyscalculia, and so far, she had been inflexible, defensive, and unwilling or unable to be curious about other methods. Perhaps, she had no choice, but our sense was that it was going to be a very long and hard journey to convince the school to offer what they simply were not equipped to provide.

The night before our IEP meeting, my husband and I decided to pull our daughter from special education math and teach her math at home. Our journey with dyscalculia had now included two different schools and two-plus years of not receiving the math help she really needed. It was time for us to find a way to teach math in a way that would connect and make sense to her dyscalculic mind.

At our IEP meeting the next morning, we sat down at the table with my daughter's three middle school teachers, her special education teacher, the student advocate, and the special education director. While they expected to discuss her IEP, we instead informed them of our new plan. We would teach our daughter's math class at home each morning and then drop her off at school for the rest of her school day.

I may have imagined it, but I am pretty sure that an expression of relief passed over the special education teacher's face. She would not have to modify her teaching methods or deal with our requests any longer. With the exception of the homeroom teacher, who was upset that my daughter would miss homeroom (the first class of the day before math), everyone else seemed fine with the plan. I shared with them briefly how my daughter's math disability would impact her performance in their classes and offered tips to help. We quickly ironed out some paperwork to dissolve the IEP, and I completed another declaration of intent to homeschool.

We immediately began our new school plan. It was a little scary to try something new but also a tremendous relief to leave behind the class experience that was causing more harm than good. We began a new way of learning math, using methods specifically for students with dyscalculia. This experience became a new adventure that turned out to be one of the best we have embarked on in our journey with dyscalculia.

chapter 6

Math for Dyscalculics

After deciding to teach my daughter math at home, the next task was finding learning material we could implement. I was already aware that math curriculum for dyscalculia did not yet exist, but I needed something to help me organize a teaching plan and prepare the lessons. I had learned enough about dyscalculia to know that we needed learning materials that were written specifically for dyscalculia. Simply using a standard math curriculum at a lower grade level would not help my daughter. While this is a common practice by special education teachers, it is not an effective method for dyscalculics.[1] Dyscalculic students do not need more of the same methods of teaching they receive in school; they need an approach unique to their specific challenges.[2]

Concrete Learning

Dyscalculia-specific learning requires the use of hands-on and concrete materials, such as glass counters, beads, dice, and dominoes. Butterworth states:[3]

> Numbers are abstract: they are abstract properties of sets, and sets themselves are abstract. However, members of sets can be concrete objects. We have found that dyscalculics are able to

make much better sense of number work when the teachers use *concrete materials* to *illustrate sets*, such as beads, counters, blocks or toys.

In traditional school settings, working with physical objects is often relegated to preschool, after which it is no longer implemented. However, the continued use of hands-on materials and objects with a strong visual impact is necessary for dyscalculics to fully understand number concepts.[4] In an interview with the Centre for Educational Neuroscience, dyscalculia expert Jane Emerson responded to a question on whether multisensory methods are a valid approach for learning disorders. The question arose after she suggested that it was essential for dyscalculics to learn through a combination of multisensory teaching along with the use of concrete materials.

I believe that the brain works as one entity with specialist areas responding more to different types of stimulations, and surely a brain that is wired differently in a dyslexic or dyscalculic learner might then select and respond to which particular modalities make sense. If you deprive a pupil from some auditory, visual or tactile inputs, then you might be removing the very modality that they *can* use to process information.[5]

Remembering how high my daughter's visual-spatial skills were in her independent educational evaluation, I figured that this method would connect for her learning style and abilities.

A Learning Plan

In searching for resources to use in a learning plan, I returned to a couple of books I had originally purchased to give to our fourth/fifth-grade special education teacher, *The Dyscalculia Toolkit* and *The Dyscalculia Resource Book*, both by Ronit Bird. However, I could not figure out how to practically use these books. While they provided learning activities and games, they did not provide a step-by-step teaching plan with sequential lessons. It seemed as if they were written for an experienced teacher, not a parent without a teaching degree.

I had also purchased an ebook by Bird, *Understanding Fractions*, to help my daughter with her math homework while she was still in the school's math class. I thought it might make sense to start our class with this ebook. I appreciated that it provided step-by-step directions on how to teach fractions. However, in the introduction, the author explained that students would need a solid understanding of multiplication and division before working through the material on fractions. If not, they should begin with the third ebook, *Understanding Times Tables*. Knowing this was our situation, I purchased the third ebook, only to find that my daughter did not have the preskills to start that ebook either. In order to start work with the times tables, she needed to have a solid grasp of step counting, doubling and halving, components, bridging, partitioning and recombining numbers, and understanding place value. Since these were not mastered concepts yet, I purchased the first two books, *Exploring Numbers Through Dot Patterns* and *Exploring Numbers Through Cuisenaire Rods*. It was then that I realized that the ebooks were a four-part series of sequential lessons that built on one another. It was the closest thing to a curriculum that I could find as they provided an overall sequential learning plan, plus teaching topics and activities that I could break into daily lessons.

Later, I discovered a more robust learning plan in *The Dyscalculia Solution: Teaching Number Sense* by Jane Emerson and Patricia Babtie, which was recommended by the staff at the Emerson House, a school in the United Kingdom that specializes in working with students with dyslexia and dyscalculia. The teaching methods and lessons in *The Dyscalculia Solution* are similar to those in Bird's ebooks, but the format is more sequential and provides clearer guidance for daily lessons.

It was a bit overwhelming to see how much my daughter lacked in her math education. I could see that she needed a solid understanding of the basics because all the other math concepts would build from there. It made sense to start at the very beginning, relearning any concepts that were confusing and filling in any comprehension gaps.

One analogy that may help explain my daughter's math situation is that of a crumbling brick wall. A wall with missing bricks and gaps in the mortar cannot sustain having new bricks added in any stable way without first being repaired, being strengthened, and having its missing pieces filled in. Our work was to start at the very beginning, at the bottom of the brick wall. As we worked our way up, we would fill in any bricks and add cement to solidify and connect concepts that were not previously joined. It might be arduous work, but I felt confident this was the way forward.

Dot Patterns and Cuisenaire Rods

We began our lessons at home with the first ebook, *Exploring Numbers Through Dot Patterns*. The focus was to become familiar and comfortable working with the numbers 1–10 at a concrete level. Bird's ebooks include an overview of the lesson's topic, an explanation of what is specifically difficult for dyscalculics, and examples of how to explain the concept in a way that connects. Some of Bird's explanations are quite lengthy, but it is evident that she has extensive experience with dyscalculic students and really understands their unique challenges. Each chapter includes videos showing how to play the various learning activities. Bird intentionally does not include any worksheets, drills, or memorization flashcards. Instead, lessons are experienced through hands-on games and activities.

For the first few math lessons, I wondered if my daughter would find the material silly or too simplistic. While the lessons were very basic, she remained interested and motivated to find a new way to learn math. She was ready to make some movement after years of confusion in math class. Almost daily, we would talk about our overall goal, which was to explore math using techniques that would make sense to the unique way she was wired. I wanted to encourage her continued engagement and ownership in the process.

After only a few lessons, we began covering concepts that seemed new to her; maybe it was just that these concepts were presented in a way that made sense to her. We learned the effective tool of using dot patterns for identifying numbers and their composition. The dot patterns 1–6 matched those of the patterns on the dice, and 7–10 were a particular combination of those initial six patterns. Dot patterns enabled my daughter to develop the ability to "see" small quantities when arranged in a recognizable pattern, without needing to count each individual dot. They also provided a new way to understand some specific math concepts in a tangible way. Later, she was able to build on this skill by visualizing the dot patterns in her mind to mentally perform simple math calculations.

After completing the first ebook on dot patterns, we moved to Bird's second ebook, *Exploring Numbers Through Cuisenaire Rods*. Cuisenaire rods are small plastic or wooden rods in colors specific to each size 1–10 cm. Each color and size corresponds to a number. A white square centimeter piece is worth "1," a 2-cm red piece is "2," the yellow piece that is 5-cm long is "5," and so on. The creator, Georges Cuisenaire, chose the particular colors using logic that conveys certain relationships between numbers.[6]

This brilliant learning tool enables the student to visualize and work with numbers greater than 10, develop a sense of numbers as quantities and not a string of ones, and build a base for later transitioning from concrete to abstract learning.[7] In this ebook, Cuisenaire rods are used to teach topics such as equations, bridging, subtraction as complementary addition, and place value. The Cuisenaire rods quickly became one of my daughter's favorite math learning tools and provided a unique way to develop her growing sense of numbers.

Common Gaps in Number Sense

There are several math concepts that are difficult for dyscalculics to grasp and, at the same time, are concepts that most educators assume a student naturally understands. These concepts may seem obvious to the average person, maybe something one just "knows." So, it might be surprising to hear that they are concepts the dyscalculic learner struggles to understand.[8] The following are a few of these concepts.

- Numbers are composed of other numbers. Another way to say this is that there are numbers inside other numbers.[9,10] For example, most people take for granted an understanding that 5 is made of 2 and 3, or 1 and 4, or even 1+1+1+1+1. But a dyscalculic does not automatically make this connection. This was one of the initial ideas explored in Bird's first two ebooks. It is a concept that requires the experience of physically adjusting objects to create quantities within other quantities. One day, my daughter was building the numbers 1–20 with the Cuisenaire rods. She quickly set up 1–10 and then asked, "How are we going to build the rest?" Then, her eyes widened in an aha moment, "All of these numbers are going to have a 10/orange rod in them, plus one other rod!" It might have been the first time she realized that all the teen numbers have a 10 in them.

- Addition is commutative. This means that no matter what order you place the numbers in, they will have the same sum. For example, 2 + 4 is the same as 4 + 2. A dyscalculic learner does not immediately understand this concept. For them, it is as if they are tackling two different problems.

- Multiplication is also commutative. The numbers can be written in either order and they will mean the same thing. But a dyscalculic has to learn this, as they will see 3 × 5 differently than 5 × 3. My daughter would see these as two separate problems and probably start with 3 × 5 because starting with the smaller number would seem less intimidating.

- Subtraction and addition are inverse operations. If 5 + 1 = 6, then it makes sense that if you start with 6 and take the 1 away, you will have 5. But subtraction is an overwhelming concept for dyscalculics, and they can struggle to imagine it. I remember showing my daughter flashcards, before we knew about her dyscalculia, and she could understand that 4 + 2 = 6, but when I immediately showed her 6 − 2 = ?, she had no idea what to do.

- Counting a group of physical items does not necessarily connect to linear counting. A dyscalculic may need to learn through experience that a group of objects will have the same number as when they are lined up on a number line or number track.[11]

- Odd and even numbers may not have any meaning attached to them. Aside from memorizing small numbers and whether they are odd or even, a dyscalculic learner will have trouble knowing which is odd or even. This important concept impacts later understanding of halving and division.[12]

- If you move one item from a set to another set, the quantity in the first set will go down by one while the other set will increase by one. This concept is what Bird calls "regrouping" and is a difficult concept for dyscalculic students to grasp.[13]

Learning that these ideas are complicated for those with dyscalculia helped me become aware of the many assumptions I had made about what I thought my daughter understood. There were reasons that seemingly simple math was so complicated for her.

Other Considerations for Dyscalculic Learning

First, successful and appropriate learning for dyscalculics also takes into consideration other difficulties particular to dyscalculia. One of these challenges is the inability to subitize. Being able to subitize, or instantly recognize small quantities without counting individually, is not an innate skill for dyscalculics, as it is for the typical person. Most people can easily subitize quantities of 1–4, and even up to 5 and 6, with great accuracy. But a dyscalculic does not even "see" these very small quantities, and they must exert great effort to learn this skill. My daughter almost never won "Connect Four" or "Pente," both games that require quick recognition of small quantities, and initially, when playing with dice, she had to count each dot to determine the quantity, even if there were only three dots. Learning dot patterns gave her some tools to help with subitizing, but this skill does not come naturally and seems to disappear and reappear at various times. It has been important for me to recognize and be patient when I notice this difficulty impacting learning or other aspects of her life.

Second, a reality that impacts dyscalculics' learning is low working memory when it comes to numbers. Because of this, dyscalculia experts frequently reiterate how important it is to limit the amount of memorization required for dyscalculic learners.[14] This stands in stark contrast to traditional teaching methods, which require memorization with a great importance placed on quick recall of math facts and procedures. For instance, there is often intense focus placed on math fluency and memorization of multiplication tables.

Removing the focus from memorization is a radically different approach to math education. But dyscalculics will benefit from an approach that requires less strain on the memory so they can focus on understanding a few key facts or basics and then use reason and logic to build from there.[15]

About a year after learning the dot patterns, when I was more familiar and patient with the memory struggles, my daughter and I were playing a dice game as a review lesson. My daughter rolled the dice, stopping and puzzling over the sum of the 6 and 4 dice. She could not recall the fact that 4 and 6 equaled 10. She began processing it out loud, "I want to start at the 6 and count up to the 4, but I know that I'm trying to work on adding without counting that way … Oh! I see a 7 and a 3, which I know is 10!" I was puzzled. Ten was the correct sum, but what did she mean by 7 and 3? Looking at the dice again, I saw what she had put together. In her mind, the 4-dot plus 3-dot pattern is something she recognizes as a "toybox" shape, the number 7. She then noticed she had 3 dots left over on the second dice. The math fact that was available to her mind in that moment was $7 + 3 = 10$, not $6 + 4$. She was able to start from something she could recall and use reason to find the solution. In a traditional math setting, an educator may have pointed out that she needed to become more fluent on the $6 + 4$ math fact; instead, we were able to call her reasoning and solution a success.

Because their working memory can be weak, the dyscalculic student will easily forget math concepts they previously mastered. Before I understood this about dyscalculia, I would become frustrated with my daughter for "forgetting" so much so easily. I would respond in unhelpful ways to her memory lapses, "Come on, you *know* this!" Now, as we experience these memory gaps, it is no longer baffling or stressful. Sometimes, when my daughter cannot recall something she has learned, she will sigh and say, "Well, there's my dyscalculia again." We understand that the lag in memory does not mean she has not learned this math fact well enough or that she is not working hard enough to remember; it is just part of having dyscalculia.

Third, dyscalculic students need a great deal more repetition and review than their peers. Rob Jennings, head of Maths and co-founder of The Dyscalculia Network, encouraged me to spend a portion of every lesson, every day, playing games that review concepts from previous lessons. The dyscalculic learner needs this consistent review in order to retain what they have learned. This requires extra patience and planning but is critical for learning success.

A Way Forward

About a month into our new math class, my daughter entered the room ready to learn and looked at me, "Mom, doing this math at home with you is fun." I was surprised. Math class, which was normally scary and stressful, was morphing into something that was actually enjoyable. For the first time, my daughter was learning to work with numbers in a way that made sense to her and she was making progress.

Meanwhile, our daily times of learning together enabled me to reach a level of understanding that I never would have attained otherwise. We often approached the lessons as if we were private detectives with a mission to uncover the mystery of how her brain worked and maybe even discover some unknown superpowers she possessed. Observing and understanding her unique struggles enabled me to explore alternative ways to solve mathematical problems with her.

Instead of feeling immediately stressed when something did not make sense, I learned to pause and wonder without judgment or frustration, "Curious. I wonder why that is?" The entire experience led to greater empathy in me and a deeper connection with my daughter, as she felt more understood and less alone in her struggles. It has also been exciting to see the progress she has made in the past two years of dyscalculia-specific math education.

About a year after we began this new way of learning math, a fellow mother of a dyscalculic child reached out to me and shared that her child was struggling with the simplicity in Bird's ebooks and felt that the math was babyish; however, the child also struggled to do the math because it was difficult. I told my daughter about this student, and she told me she remembered feeling exactly that way when she first started. She then asked if she could write them a letter, and I said, "Sure." Later that afternoon, she handed me this typed letter to send, which described her own experience and feelings.

Dear Dyscalculic Learner:

Hi, I am a dyscalculic learner just like you! I know that you might be having a hard time with relearning math a different way. You might feel like it's too babyish. I understand. When I started learning that way, and I still am, I thought it was babyish and embarrassing too. Playing with little beads on a table so you can learn how to make 10 with them while everyone else is doing arithmetic and negative numbers is frustrating, embarrassing, and sometimes lonely. Growing your math skills is going to take time. It won't be easy and there aren't any easy answers or quick fixes. Obviously, some ways of teaching will be helpful for some, but not for others. This new way could really work for you and help you in the long run, or it just won't meet your needs and that's ok! There are always good answers to our questions if we look hard enough.

Sometimes, you're gonna feel stupid. You may even feel ashamed. But ya know what? There is no shame in doing what's right for your brain and learning. We all learn in different ways and finding the way that makes sense for you is a wonderful thing! If you're like me, you went through the whole of elementary school doing math that doesn't work for you. Doing math in a way that doesn't make sense to your brain. Because of those missed years, you have to make up for them now. I promise you that doing math in a way that is helpful to you is going to help you **a lot**.

Remember that there are kids like you out there who are probably going through the same thing as you. Except they might not even know that they have dyscalculia. Sometimes, not knowing that they learn in a different way will lead them to think that they're dumb, which is really a sad thing. You are truly lucky to know what you need in order to be successful at learning.

I really do hope that this will lead you to fight for your learning and not give up 'til you have what you need.

—E. age 13

chapter 7

Anxiety and Dyscalculia

nxiety is a natural way our body can alert us when something is not right or is not safe. However, it is not healthy or sustainable for our bodies to experience high levels of anxiety on a regular basis. Dyscalculics experience a number of stresses unique to their particular situation. As parents, we can help by being aware of the causes and finding ways to help our children navigate and minimize the stress and anxiety surrounding their dyscalculia.

Often, when I find articles on how to help a child with anxiety due to learning challenges, the authors focus on simple cognitive behavioral changes and external modifications such as allowing more time for tests, getting enough sleep, having an inviting place to do homework, reducing the amount of work, offering rewards, and creating positive experiences. While these are all fine ideas, they do not explore *why* the child is experiencing anxiety so they do not deal with the causes of the discomfort. They are a sort of bandage that may make the harm less noticeable but does not ultimately help the child. While it is easier to focus on small practical ways to ease a child's anxiety, I have found it more helpful to start by digging deeper to find out what is at the root of the anxious feelings.

People experience anxiety for all sorts of reasons, many of which are socially acceptable. We expect others to feel anxious in situations such as applying for a new job, giving a presentation, taking an entrance exam, having too much to do, going through a divorce, or having a sick family member. On top of normal anxieties, a dyscalculic person faces unique anxieties from being unable to do the same things that a typical person can do without much thought or effort. A few of these everyday experiences that are extremely stressful for dyscalculics include the following:

- Being unable to remember or accurately recall personal information such as their own phone number or address, social security number, or date of birth (in digits). Fearing that if they hesitate with these numbers or need to have them written down, it will appear suspicious because it is expected that they should automatically know them.

- Struggling to understand dates given in digits, such as 5/23/21, and the inability to remember which month corresponds to which number or how many days or weeks are in a month.

- Navigating school hall situations in front of peers, such as using a locker padlock, remembering classroom numbers, struggling with directions of left and right, and not knowing how much time they have to get to class promptly.

- Situations involving telling time, such as being asked what time it is, figuring out how many minutes they have until they need to be somewhere, knowing how many hours are in a day, or figuring out how many hours an event will be when given start and end times.

- Accurately measuring, whether when baking, building, doing science experiments, or shopping for anything involving amounts.

- Wanting to buy something and not understanding how much it costs or if they have enough money for it, having a job where they have to count back change, not knowing if they give the cashier a bill whether they will receive change, or trying to calculate sale prices or tax on something they want to buy or sell.

- Needing to use their fingers to discretely count small quantities others can easily determine in their heads, hoping they never have to figure out simple subtraction in public.

- Reading a speed limit sign, understanding their speedometer, and wondering if they are going over or under the speed limit.

- Creating a budget with realistic amounts for a committee or job; understanding how to read a budget sheet to know how much money they have to spend for their project.

- Having someone ask them how much their new phone or car cost and having no idea—not even a rough estimation.

- Possessing no sense in history class whether 1796 was about the time their parents were born or a long time before; having no reference or understanding for years and their time periods.

- Saying something that sounds stupid about anything number or math related.

Not only do dyscalculics feel anxious in these everyday experiences, but they feel a pressure to hide their inabilities because they fear appearing silly. Often, they will go to great lengths to avoid situations where their struggles would be noticed. However, all the hiding and intense managing only deepens their anxiety.

These frequent stressful experiences can leave the dyscalculic feeling continually unsafe and alone. If they are not aware of their dyscalculia, or how to get help, they will form harmful internal constructs or beliefs to explain their confusing experiences. A common conclusion is, "Something is wrong with me. I must be defective or stupid and so not worthy of acceptance, love, attention, (fill-in-the-blank)."

This heartbreaking belief can be internalized by children, teens, and adults regardless of whether they are aware of their dyscalculia. Every time I spend even five minutes in one of the dyscalculia Facebook groups in which I am a member, I am presented with countless stories and expressions of this crippling belief. There are stories of adults who have felt broken and defective their entire lives, being shamed for being unable to do basic math, and who have grown up feeling they are stupid. This has limited their educational and career goals, as well as severely impacted their sense of self-worth. I also read stories of children and teens shutting down emotionally or acting out because of the belief that they are broken and unacceptable. My own daughter at age nine tearfully asked me, "Mommy, am I stupid?" as she tried to find a reason to explain why she could not do the math her friends easily could. In Samantha Abeel's memoir, *My Thirteenth Winter*, she writes about her anxiety due to her dyscalculia:

> My anxiety levels at the beginning of seventh grade were already sky-high, and I felt like a phony. I believed that if anyone found out what I couldn't do or how hard basic things like opening the locker were for me … They would think that I didn't belong. They would see the smart, wise, well-behaved, talented Sam for who she really was—a terrified, lost, inept girl.[1]

Another common belief voiced by dyscalculics is, "My inabilities in math will hold me back, and I will be limited in what I can do." They fear that their struggles will keep them from graduating from high school, getting into a good university, passing exams, being accepted for a job, or pursuing a career of interest. Unfortunately, this limiting belief can be a projection of the thoughts and feelings of the adults in the dyscalculic's life and not something that is actually true. As parents, we can easily place our own fears onto our child when we voice our concerns for their future. "If you don't get a passing grade, you'll be held back or dropped from the team." Or "You need to do well on this exam so you can get into that university." Sometimes, these beliefs spill out without us being consciously aware that we have adopted them, and they may not even be true. This pressure to meet certain standards in order to be what society considers successful only increases the dyscalculic's anxiety.

My daughter wasn't the only one with anxiety. I had my own intense feelings about her falling behind in math class. I held some strong beliefs about how doing well in school was the only way to make it in life. A deeper look revealed that my anxiety was connected to an experience I had in college. I had been stressed each year about keeping my grades up so I could finish my university degree. While my parents were able to cover a portion of my tuition, a large percentage was covered by academic scholarships. My parents had made it clear that I could not take on any debt for school, so I relied heavily on these scholarships. Receiving low grades in any class could mean losing a scholarship, which could mean leaving the university. When I was able to recognize this subconscious belief about what it meant to not do well in school, I could see that my anxiety was from my own story and I could untangle those anxious feelings from my daughter's situation.

How to Help

Prolonged and ongoing experiences of stress and trauma can cause irreversible harm to the mind and body, which is why we must alleviate the causes of anxiety for our dyscalculic loved ones. While some anxiety will always be present in life, the harmful and crippling anxiety so many dyscalculics face does not need to be a reality in their life just because they are dyscalculic. There are ways to address the deep beliefs causing anxiety and to become aware of areas where reoccurring trauma can be limited. The following are five actions that have been immensely helpful in reducing my daughter's anxiety, as well as my own anxiety as a parent.

Action 1: Seek help for our own anxiety first.

As a psychotherapist, my husband often receives calls from parents who are concerned and looking into therapy options for their child. In most cases, once he meets with the family, it is evident that the parents are holding a great deal of their own unexamined anxieties and past traumas. It is difficult for parents to admit that perhaps their own mental health is impacting their child's well-being. They simply want their child's emotional problems to be alleviated without having to do their own inner work. I know several fellow parents whose children suffered from debilitating anxieties, making it almost impossible to get them out the door for school. These parents first looked into several therapeutic options for their children and received a few cognitive behavioral tools to help cope with the anxiety, but the results were not significant. It was not until these parents received their own consistent therapy and support that their children's anxieties began to noticeably lessen.

Children are intuitively in sync with and emotionally connected to their parents. They have a sort of invisible sonar to our emotions and feelings, regardless of whether we recognize the feelings in ourselves. Recently, one of my daughters said to me, "I feel stressed, and I don't know why." I stopped rushing around and paused to consider her comment. I realized that my husband and I were stressed about a particular situation, and it was this stress that our daughter was internalizing. Once we were able to name that stress as our own, my daughter's stress was immediately alleviated. Children are especially vulnerable to picking up on the unspoken fears of adults and then adopting them as their own.

Another way our own unexamined anxieties can impact our children is through our projection of those fears. I remember, before we knew about our daughter's dyscalculia, sometimes feeling she was being lazy or not working hard enough, which I assumed could be a reason for her math struggles. Interestingly enough, this fear of being perceived as lazy or not working hard enough was a fear I had carried most of my life. In these moments, I was projecting my own internal fears onto my daughter as a way to rid myself of the parts in myself I did not like, parts I considered lazy. I, instead, was telling myself that it was my daughter who was being lazy. This was obviously damaging and untrue.

It is from my own experience that I make this suggestion to become aware of and receive support for your own anxieties first. It is similar to putting on your own oxygen mask before putting one on your child. I would not be able to do the important work of supporting my daughter with her anxiety without weekly dealing with my own anxieties, past traumas, and limiting beliefs. Examining one's own anxieties is complicated and messy work. This is why most parents hope they can start somewhere else, someplace easier. However, to get to the bottom of the anxiety in any real way, this deep inner work is essential. I recommend getting help from a trained and experienced professional.

Action 2: Talk openly about dyscalculia and continue to learn more together.

It baffles me that there are parents who do not want their child to know that the latter has dyscalculia because they are afraid that their child will feel bad about themself. This thinking is most likely a product of the parents' own unexamined blocks or fears surrounding what it means to be dyscalculic. I would argue that it is important for the child to know about their dyscalculia so they can better understand themselves and what they need to be successful in life. Butterworth writes in *Dyscalculia: From Science to Education*:

> I am often told by educationalists that it is bad to "label" people. All the dyscalculics I have worked with tell me that it is far, far better to be labelled dyscalculic than to be labelled stupid, not only because of the ways others see them, but, perhaps more importantly, how they see themselves.[2]

When I began talking with my daughter about our suspicion that she may have dyscalculia, and then continued talking with her after she had an official diagnosis, her anxiety decreased dramatically. There was finally a reason for her confusion and struggles. This knowledge was empowering for her. We continued to learn together about how dyscalculia would impact her learning and her life. This also normalized dyscalculia as a unique way that a segment of the population processes numbers.

Now as a teen she sometimes laughs about her situation or cracks jokes about her own dyscalculia. Certain aspects of life are still very hard, especially math class, but the level of overall anxiety is much lower. She has a reason for why numbers are difficult, and because she has a terminology for and growing understanding of her situation, she is able to self-advocate when she needs to. She also feels less alone, which has led to her increased empathy for others who are neurodiverse.

Action 3: Build trust and connection by working through tough emotions.

Trust is built when we provide a consistent safe place for our children to be their full selves. Being able to talk openly about difficult things and share any feelings (even the uncomfortable ones) is critical for creating a supportive environment in which our children can thrive.

It is vital for our children's health that they be able to voice their feelings and engage with us as they work through their emotions. If they are not provided this opportunity, they will find other ways to express their anxiety and other intense emotions. The body cannot hold on to these unresolved feelings, so if anxiety cannot be released and communicated safely, it will manifest in the form of nail biting, nervous twitches, repetitive movement, neck tension, headaches, stomachaches, and other bodily expressions.

It is not always easy for us as parents to allow children to express their feelings, especially if the emotions are ones with which we are uncomfortable. For me, a hard one is anger. I struggle with being okay with my own anger or experiencing the anger of others. My instinctual response when one of my daughters expresses anger or frustration is to try to put an end to it. We all have certain emotions that can trigger us and make us feel uncomfortable; instead of anger, some may be triggered by sadness or disappointment. It helps to be aware of these tricky emotions and to work through our own issues with them. That way, we can allow our children to express whatever emotions come up within them and help them work through their feelings.

I have a tendency toward fixing problems in a practical way. It feels natural for me to respond with a seemingly helpful tip or piece of advice to something my daughter is sharing with me instead of paying attention to the emotion behind what she is saying. But that is almost never what my daughter is looking for. What she needs is not my help fixing a problem but a place to work out the *feelings* she is experiencing because of the problem. One way I know this is true is that even if I provide a perfectly good solution to the problem, the difficult emotion is still in the room. As they have grown older, my daughters will sometimes say to me, "I don't need you to fix the problem. I just need you to listen." This is still challenging for me, even after years of therapy and practicing this new skill. In an effort to empathize with the feeling rather than solve the problem, these are some of the go-to phrases I try to remember:

- That *is* really hard.

- I can see why that is so frustrating/sad/stressful/annoying.

- You must feel scared/upset/angry.

When I can allow the feelings, and not try to dismiss them or fix the problem, I find that my daughters and I are able to work through the moment more easily and end up at a place that is more connected. The bonus is that, usually, we also experience a sense that the problem itself has been resolved, even if it is just the emotions that have been worked through and the problem actually still exists.

Action 4: Question situations or norms causing anxiety and make necessary changes.

Addressing anxiety involves a balance of working through the inner world while also looking at the environmental stressors that are creating repeated trauma. While we are helping our child heal from internal beliefs that cause anxiety, we can also take a look at their learning environment and make changes to benefit their well-being. We cannot expect their anxiety to lessen if we are repeatedly placing them in anxiety-producing situations where they continue to experience new trauma. Many dyscalculics are continually pushed to make it through the school system the best they can. We should not be surprised that they continue to develop increasingly higher levels of anxiety or that they begin to shut down from feeling overwhelmed.

There are many practical choices parents can make to alleviate the sources of stress in their dyscalculic's school life. Sometimes, these are small tweaks; other times, an overhaul of the educational setting is needed. It is important that parents feel unafraid to challenge the norm when it does not allow their child to grow. Having a child with unique needs means that they are most likely going to need a unique plan for learning success. They are not going to thrive in the same environment or within the same system as their nondyscalculic peers. As parents, it is our responsibility to make the adjustments needed and embrace ways that may be outside the box.

One pivot I made early on was to opt my daughter out of any state or school district standardized math testing. She would experience overwhelming anxiety leading up to the testing days and during the testing, and she was completely exhausted afterward. No assistance was allowed during the tests, so my daughter's stress grew even more intense because the monitors would not answer any questions she had when she was completely lost. Sometimes, she would end up choosing random answers on the test because that was the only option available to her. With the increased levels of anxiety, the rest of the school day was wasted because she could not focus on learning after the taxing experience. I decided it did not make sense for my daughter to experience this level of anxiety for the benefit of the school or state, so we opted out of the math portions each time the tests came around. I received some pushback from the school personnel, who wanted full participation for the tests, but I insisted that we would not be putting our daughter through these unnecessary anxiety-producing evaluations.

Another change I made that has reduced anxiety considerably, both for myself and my daughter, was to remove the pressure for her to be at a certain level or to keep up with the common core curriculum in math. This has freed her up to learn at a pace that makes sense for her given her dyscalculia. By teaching her math at home, and later fully homeschooling her, we were able to find systems with which she achieved success. Not being under so much stress to keep up has allowed her to set benchmarks and even enjoy math learning. My overall goal is for her to learn the basics of math and to progress as far as she can with the dyscalculic learning material. As she moves into high school in the next couple of years, we will focus on the practical application of math in life, such as all aspects of working with money, managing and tracking time, using a calculator effectively with estimation as a checking tool, and measurements.

There is a lot of pressure on parents to have their students keep up with the school system, and I wonder for what reason. Does this pressure benefit the child? Does it help them flourish and learn? Does it help them get into a great school or obtain a fulfilling career? No, it does not. But it sure creates more anxiety. And one thing we know about anxiety is that it shuts down our capacity to learn and develop.

I recently spoke with a local dyscalculia tutor, who told me that her most important work was helping students regain their confidence and easing the anxiety they face with math. She told me that there are usually two types of parents. One group wants their child to grow in their understanding of math, make progress from wherever they are, and feel supported and confident. The other group of parents is primarily concerned that their child keeps up with the class, gets their homework in on time, and passes the school exams. The children of the parents in this second group have a difficult time progressing because of crippling anxiety and the pressure to move at a pace that does not work for them, to memorize information they cannot apply, and to push through arbitrary standards that do not account for their situation. Meanwhile, it is the children of the parents in the first group who are more likely to make the most progress in their math understanding.

Action 5: Look for the gold and let it shine.

As a parent, it is easy to become focused on what is going wrong or what needs work. As someone who resonates with the Enneagram 1 personality type,[3] the reformer in me is constantly looking for what needs to be made better. I spend more time trying to fix what is not working than I do looking for what is working well and encouraging more of those things. Susan Wise Bauer writes in her book *Rethinking School*:

> The tendency is to focus on the child's *slower* areas, to spend more time on those in order to move the child into a higher grade. But the result can be that the child ends up evaluating himself by his weaknesses, not his strengths. And this can obscure natural gifts, requiring children to spend untold hours laboring away at subjects they dislike, at the expense of learning in which they excel.[4]

Regardless of whether your child is 2e, each child has their own areas in which they shine—in which they have a special interest, a talent, or a natural gift. Bauer is right. If the focus remains mostly on the areas that need work, our children will begin to identify with those, instead of finding confidence and motivation in the areas in which they excel. It is just as critical to develop these areas of interest and excellence in our kids as it is to help them with those with which they struggle.

For my daughter, this has meant supporting her passion for art, painting, drawing, writing, bird watching, and being in nature, all of which bring her joy. These activities also build her confidence in who she is, giving her the necessary tools to handle the more difficult aspects of her life. Growing in the areas she considers her "superpowers" has increased her excitement about learning and has led her to be more aware of herself and others. She is, in fact, not broken or defective; she is a wonder and an inspiration.

chapter 8

Practical Support at Home

Sometimes when I choose to share about my daughter's math learning disability, the response is something along the lines of, "Well, good thing she can just use a phone calculator." Inside, I am thinking, "If only living with dyscalculia was made easier by simply using a phone calculator!" I know the person with whom I am speaking means to be encouraging and that they are unaware of how dyscalculia impacts multiple aspects of a person's life, but this is still a frustrating experience.

While the most effective ways to help a child with dyscalculia are to minimize anxiety and to use dyscalculia-specific methods for learning math, there are also some practical ways to provide further support at home.

As my understanding of dyscalculia has grown, I have begun to notice everyday situations that are impacted by having this disability. It helps to share these observations with my daughter to confirm what I am noticing. In this way, I learn more about her experience as someone disconnected to numbers and she learns more about how others who are not dyscalculic may experience the same situation differently. Sometimes, just this awareness on both our parts is helpful enough. Other times, we will come up with an alternative method if some-

thing is problematic for her. While I share some of the adjustments
our family has made in our home life to better support our differently
wired daughter, my hope is that they spur your own ingenuity as you
seek solutions for your own family.

Awareness with Games

As our girls have grown older, it has been fun to expand our family
game options from Chutes and Ladders and Candy Land to more
interesting and involved board games. One family favorite is The Settlers of Catan.

A couple of years ago, while our family was playing Settlers, our
dyscalculic daughter was feeling repeatedly flustered and unsure what
to do on her turn. Her distress was noticeable and impacted how
much fun we all had playing. After losing with a much lower score
than the rest of the family, she vented, "I don't like this game. Why
do I always lose when we play it?" She was right. She never did well at
the game; even her younger sister was much better at it. I remember
she crawled into my husband's lap for a comforting snuggle, and I
pulled out my laptop to search "strategy games and dyscalculia." In
the results, I found evidence that dyscalculia did seem to impact the
ability to play many games, but I could not find a reason for why this
particular game was difficult. Some dyscalculics suffer from low executive function skills so the planning is a struggle in some games, but
this did not seem to match my daughter's situation with her above-
average problem-solving and critical-reasoning skills. It was not until
a year later that I realized *why* this particular game was so difficult.
I was writing a blog post about the inaccurate assumptions we make
about what dyscalculics know. Then, it hit me. The math involved in
this game seemed so simple that I had not considered the possibility
that my daughter was unable to do the basic calculations as quickly
as the rest of the family. In fact, I had not even thought of the score-

keeping involved as "math." As I saw it through my daughter's eyes, I realized it was actually quite complicated for her to track.

The goal of the game is to be the first person to reach 10 points. Points are gained through various acquisitions, each with its own point value. A settlement is worth 1 point, and there are 5 settlements available. A city is worth 2 points, with a maximum of 4 cities available. The Longest Road or Largest Army card is worth 2 points, and Victory Point cards are worth 1 point. To play the game, each player needs to keep track of how many points they have on the board, how many points each of their opponents have, how many points are needed to win, and how many cities or settlements are available to put into play. While the typical person can quickly recognize all of these things, this calculating process requires a great deal of focus and energy for someone with dyscalculia. In order to understand all of these moving parts, my daughter's mental calculations would probably go something like this:

> Let's see, I have 3 settlements, so that is 3 points. Plus, 2 cities, and they are 2 each, so let's see, I have 4 city points. Now how many settlements did I have? Oh yeah, 3. So I have 3 and 4 and so I have 1, 2, 3, 4, 5, 6, 7 (counting on fingers from beginning), so I have 7. Oh, but I have the Longest Road card, so that is another 2. What is 7 plus 2. Oh no! It's my turn to roll and I haven't finished counting my points. Oh well, I guess I'll just buy another development card because I have the cards for that.

No wonder she was so frustrated when playing this game. Trying to keep track of her own points plus everyone else's required so much effort. It was sad because the rest of us enjoyed the game and she enjoyed all the other aspects of the game that were not related to numbers.

When I came to this realization, I ran my wonderings by her. She gave me a big hug. "Yes! That is exactly how it is!" I understood the hug to mean that she felt loved that I understood why the game was hard, even when she did not know herself. Now that we could see why the difficulty was there, we were able to come up with something that has helped her enjoy the game, and even win sometimes. She needed both a concrete way to see how many points each person had without having to work so hard to add them and a way to quickly calculate her own points. To address this issue, I created laminated scorecards for each person to keep track of their points. The winning 10 points were depicted in the shape of the 10-dot pattern my daughter was now familiar with. The card was placed face up for everyone else to see and we used our white board markers to fill in points gained and erase points taken away. This small change has made a world of difference.

Having a dyscalculic family member does not mean we need to avoid games with numbers; we just need to be aware of the differences and patient as those individuals work with any numbers or perform calculations. I have noticed that scorekeeping is less complicated when it can be easily deciphered as one moves along a track.

Another game our family plays is Qwixx, a dice game. It is fun, is easy to play, and is also a powerful learning game for dyscalculics who have mastered their dot patterns. When we play as a family, I have had to remind my husband and our younger daughter to not jump in with the dice sums when it is not their turn. They can quickly see the totals, but it takes our dyscalculic daughter a bit more time to sum the dice. Sometimes, she will self-advocate and remind us to keep the total to ourselves because she wants to determine or sum the numbers herself.

Time and Do-It-Yourself Clocks

Telling time and understanding time calculations are areas for which we are always looking for creative support. One of my daughter's favorite tools is a clock that we modified in a way that is easier for her to read; each hour is designated a different pie-shaped color and each hour number is placed in the center of the pie-shaped wedge. One of the problems with regular analog clocks is that the number is shown at the beginning of the hour and at the outer edge, so it is not clear to dyscalculics that the whole area between the numbers belongs to the first hour. We created our modified clock using a simple analog clock from Target. It was important that the clock face not be covered in glass, and it helped that it did not have numbers on the face. (Any clock with an uncovered face can be used and numbers can be covered up if they are flat on the clock surface.) I cut out pie-shaped pieces of construction paper and glued them to the clock face, and my daughter wrote the hour in the middle of each pie-hour. She also placed the minutes around the outer edge. She has this clock in her room and uses it daily to tell time. To see a picture of this clock, visit my website.[1]

Another tool we use regularly to help with time is a Time Timer.[2] (We have an old one from the girl's toddler years, but Time Timer now makes a variety of sizes and styles, including a phone app.) We have been using this for years and it greatly helps my daughter to see how much time she has left to complete a task or to get ready to go somewhere. If you are not familiar with a Time Timer, it is a visual timer that shows how much time is left in a 60-minute time frame, with a red-colored area that shrinks as the time goes by. The Time Timer has equal spacing for each minute, so it moves at the same speed the entire time, as opposed to an hourglass, which appears to move faster as it reaches the narrow opening at the bottom.

You may wonder why a dyscalculic cannot just use a digital timer, with the numbers moving backward until they reach zero. The answer is that a digital timer is not visual enough. For a dyscalculic, it is a stressful screen of flashing numbers and does not help them understand how far away from zero they are.

The most frequent use of our Time Timer happens when we are about to leave the house. This was an area of frequent frustrations until we figured out a few helpful changes. I realized that my daughter's lack of an internal sense of time contributed to the problem, as well as her inability to determine how long it would take to do everything she needed to do before leaving. Because she was not able to quickly tell time on a clock and easily calculate the remaining minutes, she was often stressed about getting ready and we were stressed because of how long it was taking her. Now, when she uses the Time Timer to give a visual of the time before we leave (I usually tell her how long we have), and makes herself a list of all the things she needs to do, we are able to get out the door more on time and with less stress. Sometimes, she still needs help determining how long a certain task will take if it is something she does not regularly do.

There is an excellent TEDx Talk on YouTube from a student in Denmark who is dyscalculic. She shares how she came up with a way to make sure she arrived to school on time by listening to the same playlist each day, the duration of which was the exact amount of time she needed to make her commute. This is a brilliant idea that could be applied to other situations, especially if your child loves music.[3]

Making Sense of Schedules, Planners, and Dates

My family sometimes teases me for my love of creating schedule spreadsheets. They are colorful, with the days of the week on top, all the hours of the day down the side, and each type of activity a different color. I tried making one of these once for my dyscalculic daughter, but it proved unhelpful. I tried posting the family schedule on the wall so she could see when everything was happening. I hoped to get a break from questions such as "When is dinner?" or "When do we leave for school?" or "When does Dad get home?" It took me a long while to notice that she never seemed to reference the posted schedule. One day, during a conversation over school schedules, she told me that she found the spreadsheet very confusing. To her, it was difficult to read and translate. This surprised me. I thought it was basic and self-explanatory, clear enough even for a dyscalculic. I was wrong. It was overwhelming for her to decode, which is why she avoided it altogether. We needed another way for her to understand where in the day she was and to be able to see what was happening next.

The idea came to me that maybe we could use another of the wood clocks from Target and modify it for a day's schedule. The hour hand could show where in the day the current time was. The pie-shaped segments of time could be applied with double-sided tape so they could be easily modified depending on the current season's schedule. For this version of the clock, I cut off the second hand near its base and later cut down the minute hand as well. The schedule clock only showed 12 hours, 9:00 a.m.–9:00 p.m., but for our daughter's schedule, that was all we needed. Our daughter is able to get up with her natural internal clock at 9:00 a.m., a perk of being home-schooled. After 9:00 p.m., she does not generally need to know what part of the day it is as we are having family time, reading, and getting ready for bed. For pictures of and instructions for making this clock, visit my website.[4]

On one recent Saturday, our family was tackling some chores together around the house. My daughter was agitated more than usual about Saturday chores. She told me that she did not know if she would have any time to work on an art project she was involved with. She wondered if the whole day would be used up by chores. I told her we would only be working for an hour or so, but that did not help her. I pulled out this clock and visibly showed her where in the day we were and how much time she had left over the rest of the day to work on her art. "Oh!" she replied. "Yes, that is plenty of time." She was relieved to see a picture of the day and her agitation at the chores diminished. She knew when she would get to do art and how long she had to work on it; she had needed to visually see it, not just hear it in numbers that meant nothing to her.

As we moved to homeschooling full time during the COVID-19 pandemic, we had to find a practical way for our daughter to track what projects and classwork she needed to complete each day. My original plan was to set up our day similarly to a traditional school day with hours set aside for specific subjects. However, this broken-up routine quickly became frustrating for my daughter. She did not think of her day in hour increments, so it was unnatural for her to constantly be checking the clock and switching subjects because the schedule was set that way. Our advisor suggested that we move to a different model, perhaps doing one subject per day. This was a brilliant idea that my daughter quickly embraced. We would do math every day, but the other subjects were divided over the week so she could devote an entire day to one subject. Instead of an hour schedule to follow with times, she made herself a weekly checklist of what projects and activities she would work on each day. This was her version of a weekly planner. For events that were out of the ordinary, such as a planned hangout with a friend or a Zoom class, she would set an alarm on her device as a reminder. We also created some space in her Friday schedule to catch up on anything she missed during the week. This new routine has worked really well for someone who lives mostly unaware of time. She has also learned to take more ownership of her schedule, and I just check in occasionally to make sure it matches up with our monthly goals for learning.

Another tricky piece about schedules and planning is that dates in digit form can be complicated for dyscalculics to translate accurately. When my daughter was still in public school, she would often scramble to complete homework at the last minute or the night before. It was not until I was observing her one day that I realized she did not have an understanding of the due dates written at the top of her assignments. Pointing to the date at the top of her assignment, I remarked, "It says right there that it is due tomorrow. How did you miss this until now?" She told me that those numbers did not help her because she did not know what they meant. She only copied due dates such as "4/13/20" because those were what the teacher wrote on the board. I am not sure how we missed this several years into our dyscalculia journey. But, of course, it made sense that digits would be complicated for a dyscalculic to understand. One way to stay more on top of things could be for me to check my daughter's homework all the time, but I feel she needs to take primary responsibility over her work. Upon further discussion, she and I determined there was a method that made more sense to her and would allow better tracking of due dates. If the teacher said, "This is due next Wednesday," my daughter could imagine what that meant, so she started writing "Due next Wednesday" on her homework and told the teacher that doing so helped her manage homework due dates. It was simple but helpful. The number of last-minute homework assignments dropped when she could think in terms of days of the week, instead of tracking digits.

Another story about date confusion occurred regarding a TV show. Our family had been watching (don't laugh!) *Curse of Oak Island* on the History Channel. But I noticed that my dyscalculic daughter did not enjoy it as much as the rest of us. As we were watching one evening, it occurred to me one possible factor hindering her enjoyment of the show was that she had no context for the dates that were constantly being discussed. The treasure hunters would talk about specific dates, which gave them context for their finds. Often, they would be excited about an artifact that was from a specific time period because there was meaning attached to that period. But this meaning was completely missed by my daughter, who only heard a string of numbers. When I realized this, I quickly jotted down a timeline for her showing the main dates in the story. Then, when a new date came up on the show, I pointed on the visual timeline to the year or time period they were referencing. "Oh!" she exclaimed a few times when she recognized the significance of the date. This did not make the show anywhere near her favorite, but when we did watch, she had more of an understanding of what was happening.

Cooking and Baking

During the pandemic, my younger daughter took up baking as a hobby to help ease her loneliness and the sadness she felt at being away from all her friends. One day, she was showing her older sister how to make chocolate mug cakes. As my younger daughter talked aloud about the measurements needed for each of their mug cakes, my older daughter, who had become overwhelmed by all the numbers, blurted out, "I'll just take your word for it."

Shortly after this interaction, I was cooking dinner with my dyscalculic daughter and was reminded again how difficult cooking could be for her as we had to translate liquid ounces to cups, double the recipe, and make adjustments to amounts based on substitutions we needed to make. When we were finished, she looked exhausted. This time, she was the one who came up with an idea to relieve the struggle. She told me she would like to make her own recipe notebook with simple recipes she could easily understand and follow. She wanted to feel more confident with cooking, and less scared. I thought this was an excellent idea. It could really enable her to feel confident about cooking for herself and for others instead of throwing out the option of cooking because of the stress it causes.

Another tool we recently discovered is visual measuring spoons and measuring cups from Welcome Industries.[5] They have created a set of measuring tools that visually represent the actual amounts. One-half of a teaspoon is literally half of a circle. One-fourth of a cup is a pie wedge that is a quarter of the cup size. Usually, my daughter spends a great deal of time rummaging in the drawer to find the matching fraction on the handle of the spoon or cup to match the one in the recipe. Now, when she bakes cookies with her new measuring spoons, she can quickly grab the correct tool because of the clear visual representation.

Number Sequences

It was soon after we discovered our daughter's dyscalculia that we purchased a bike for her birthday, along with a basket and lock. I knew she would have trouble remembering the lock combination because number sequences are extremely difficult for dyscalculics to recall, so we purchased a bike lock that opened with a word. She has had no trouble remembering this word, while I know remembering a code would have been almost impossible.

Another tool we have used in the past to help with number sequencing is music. When I was still focused on helping her memorize her multiplication tables (I am no longer), I would find songs to help with the skip count steps. To this day, she can still recall the songs for counting by 3s, 4s, and 6s. It remained difficult for her to connect these memorized songs to understanding her times tables, but the method did help her to remember a string of numbers. Similarly, she has been able to recall some math procedures when they are put to song; for example, her third-grade teacher taught her a little jingle to remember how to round a number, and she still repeats it whenever she is faced with that task.

Be a Resource to Others

Another way to help your child when they are facing a situation in which their dyscalculia will impact everyday life experiences is by advocating in situations outside of the home and helping your child advocate for themselves.

Whenever my daughter joins a class, I think through where her dyscalculia will cause difficulties and let the teacher know about her situation so that they can be helpful and not put my daughter on the spot or ridicule her for not being able to do something most students can. When she recently signed up for a creative writing class on imaginary worlds, I noticed one session was on timelines and dates so a simple email let the teacher know this area might be a struggle for my daughter. For science class, we notified the teacher of the areas that would be challenging, such as experiments involving measurements or tracking time.

I recently realized what a nightmare tracking tennis scores would be for a dyscalculic. Love, 15, 30, 40 (What?!), not to mention remembering the numbers and where one is at so you can announce the score at each turn. I continue to find new situations that would be confusing as a dyscalculic, and my empathy grows.

As I look ahead at my daughter's journey, I know some outside-the-box thinking will be required to help her with navigating high school class schedules, driving a car, handling money, being on time to her first job, and many other aspects of everyday life. But I also know that if I continue to keep an open mind and collaborate with her to look for creative solutions, there is no challenge that cannot be overcome or at least eased.

chapter 9

Raising Awareness

Personal stories open my eyes and enlighten me. When others share their unique experiences, it widens my perspective. This is how we can raise awareness for dyscalculia in our communities. By sharing our own stories with authenticity, we plant seeds of understanding. My hope is that putting forth our family's experience with dyscalculia will contribute to growing the movement started by those who have already bravely shared their own experiences, individuals such as Samantha Abeel (through her memoir)[1] and Line Rothmann (through her TEDx Talk).[2] Sometimes, even just a little movement can put entire systems into motion.

When I learned that about 5% of the population, or 1 in every 20 persons, is dyscalculic, I realized that there must be more dyscalculics around me than just my daughter. Most likely they are already in my social circles, maybe unaware that their number difficulties are because of a learning disability. Or they are keeping their dyscalculia hidden.

My husband has a friend who could very possibly be dyscalculic. As long as they have known each other, this friend has displayed often frustrating behaviors that are always explained away as "that's just the way he is." One day, as my husband and I were talking about this friend's particular struggles and how they were impacting their friendship, a thought hit me and I said to my husband, "Could he be dyscalculic?" As we talked further, my husband recalled how this friend had failed his college math class, was often late or would not show up for events, and would get lost and confused with directions. My husband commented how much more empathy he felt knowing these behaviors could be because of dyscalculia and not because his friend was simply thoughtless or irresponsible. Later, the two of them ended up talking about the possibility of dyscalculia, which was something his friend had never heard of. This friend opened up to share other struggles related to numbers: his lack of understanding of the family finances, how he struggled with budgets at work, and how he was sometimes stressed when ordering coffee because of the various sizes. As my husband showed his friend some woodworking projects he was completing, his friend commented how he had always been interested in working with wood but could never understand measurements enough to try it.

My husband's friend is an example of someone possibly living with dyscalculia, unaware there could be a reason for their challenges. In an attempt to avoid ridicule by others, he masked his struggles with humor and feigned ignorance. Dyscalculics are all around us, often living in shame or silence. It is critical that we become aware of how life is for them and work to include and support them in our number-saturated world.

Awareness and Advocacy in School

Brian Butterworth presents the idea that dyscalculic learners should be recognized as early as kindergarten.[3] If this is the case, then we need to begin identifying children who exhibit symptoms of dyscalculia at a much earlier age so they can be offered immediate support and differentiated learning that will help them be successful in school. As it is now, we wait years before diagnosing a child's learning needs.

By that time, they have already begun to develop detrimental beliefs about themselves and their abilities that are hard to undo.

It is frustrating how little training there is for educators when it comes to learning disabilities, especially when they could be the first to notice them. Teachers need to receive education on how to recognize students with specific learning challenges. Special education teachers must be made aware of particular nuances and best teaching practices related to dyscalculics. These learning methods will not only benefit those with dyscalculia but also others with learning difficulties such as dyslexia.

Universities need to offer courses on dyscalculia for teachers in their initial and continuing education programs. A few universities in the United Kingdom are already doing so.[4] If universities offer programs on dyscalculia, then educational psychologists, who diagnose learning disabilities, will gain increased awareness of dyscalculia. Universities can also help further the research on the causes, symptoms, early intervention options, and effective teaching methods related to dyscalculia.

Change with Government Policies

Government policies on education need reform so that they recognize and support those with dyscalculia. Policies that inhibit dyscalculics from learning about their disability or receiving the help they need must be removed and policies for the support of dyscalculics implemented. In the United States, we have a start with the IDEA, but further work is necessary as many of the ideals in this law do not trickle down to the student's level. How the law is implemented varies from state to state and from school district to school district, dependent on how the law is interpreted at the local level. For example, the IDEA ensures that all parents are allowed to request a learning disability evaluation for their child. But if only the teacher, and not the parents, is aware of the learning disability, this child will never receive an evaluation because the teacher is not allowed to freely share their concerns and observations with the parents without fear of a lawsuit. The IDEA also states that if a school is unable to provide the suitable assistance a student needs for their learning disability, then it must provide funds for the student to get learning support elsewhere. Yet, at a practical level, this rarely works out because it involves expensive legal battles to prove that the school is not providing adequate or needed support for the child. Systems such as this are broken and need to be repaired.

Our institutions of government and education are not likely to become more aware of dyscalculia on their own. Bringing light to this disability is going to require parents and students with dyscalculia to take the initiative and insist on the necessary changes, banding together through groups and associations to make our voices heard.

Societal Awareness

Garnering attention will take more people sharing their personal stories and being willing to speak up for loved ones with dyscalculia. This requires us paying attention as we volunteer in schools, as we go to our places of work, and as we contribute to conversations with neighbors and friends.

I have a friend who is a social worker in one of our local hospitals. This past year, she had been treating a young mom at risk of losing custody of her baby. The baby was suffering from severe malnutrition, and the new mom seemed to have marked difficulty with tracking time and measurements. The mother was unable to tell the doctors how many ounces of formula she had mixed or how much the baby had consumed, and she could not tell what time, even an estimation, of when the baby had last been fed. While the typical medical professional might assume the mother was irresponsible, thoughtless, or unfit to care for her infant, my friend considered another possibility. She suspected that the young mom may be dyscalculic. She had been following my blog and recognized what could be symptoms of dyscalculia, such as an inability to understand measurements and ratios for mixing formula, lack of awareness of timing and frequency of feeding, trouble estimating amounts, and memory weakness for numbers. When this social worker friend recognized these behaviors as possible symptoms of dyscalculia, she was able to approach the situation in a new way and help her patient by making adjustments and accommodations for the baby's care plan so that the mom could provide adequate nourishment for her baby. This level of awareness of the symptoms and impact of dyscalculia is needed in our society. It is stories like this one, with possible severe consequences, that convey the urgency with which we must grow our awareness.

There are countless stories online of adults who have been unable to perform their jobs or even apply for a job because of their fear of what others would think of their lack of acuity with numbers. I cannot help but wonder if this anxiety could be alleviated if dyscalculia was something more of us were aware of and was something that was socially understood. Perhaps those with dyscalculia would then be free to share about their disability and get the help they need. Can you imagine a world in which a dyscalculic could say to a stranger, "Excuse me, can you help me figure out this bus schedule? I am dyscalculic." Or, even say to friends, "Hey, can you help me total this bill? My dyscalculia is tripping me up again." Think how liberating it could be for dyscalculics to freely admit to the world that they are dyscalculic and not be shamed or ridiculed but, instead, be met with understanding.

Growing Our Curiosity and Openness

When my daughter was nine years old, she reached her own conclusion of what was causing her math struggles: "Mommy, I know what has happened. My creative, artistic, imaginative part of my brain is so big that it has pushed out the math part; there just is not enough room for it." She was probably right.

As our society grows in awareness of this unique demographic, other questions come to mind: "What unique perspective does a dyscalculic offer that we could learn from? What would happen if we were open and curious about their way of operating in the world? What if we inquired about their unique perspective, instead of just trying to fix them or force them to adapt to the majority? Recently, I read a story about how the Government Communications Headquarters in the United Kingdom hires individuals with dyslexia because of their highly capable and unique skills in espionage.[5] Dyslexics can often see patterns and decode some messages better than the average person. Their disability has become a superpower. I cannot help but wonder what unique possibilities there are for dyscalculics? Can they see things in a way that a nondyscalculic person cannot?

This past year, our homeschool advisor asked if we were familiar with the Mayan number system, and out of curiosity, I looked it up. The system is much different than our Arabic number system. I decided to print out the numbers 0–19 and cut them into individual cards. Then, I gave them to my dyscalculic daughter and told her that they were Mayan numbers and asked if she could put them in order. While I expected her to love the challenge, I did not expect her to solve it as fast as she did. In about a minute, she had sorted them and lined them all up correctly; then, she explained the logic of how she thought the system worked. She was correct on everything. This intrigued me, so I furthered the experiment by giving the same activity to my other daughter who does well in math in school and is not dyscalculic. She did not have the same experience. She struggled for several minutes and repeatedly asked me for hints. Finally, she lined them up in a pattern that was incorrect. Her comment was, "Wow, these are so confusing! I'm glad our number system makes much more sense." My dyscalculic daughter looked up thoughtfully and asked, "Do you think the numbers made sense to me because I see numbers a different way?" I honestly do not know the answer to her question, and this was obviously not a large enough test group to draw any sort of conclusion. But it is intriguing that a neurotypical child found something confusing that the dyscalculic found intuitive and clear.

I wonder what else we will uncover about the dyscalculic mind with just a little curiosity and openness.

Conclusion

One late autumn morning, my daughter and I sat down at the coffee table for our daily math lesson. I noticed that she seemed distracted, her head down as she absentmindedly fiddled with the Cuisenaire rods.

"What are you thinking about?" I prompted.

She looked up with a somber expression and told me she had been wondering what to say when the kids at school asked why she was doing math class at home instead of with them. She felt upset at the thought that the other kids might think she wasn't smart enough to be in their math class.

We sat in silence. I had to consciously remind myself to be in the moment with her and to listen to her thoughts and feelings without rushing in to fix anything.

"That's really hard," I responded. "I can see why you don't know how to explain to the other kids where you are during math class, especially at a new school when you are just making friends."

We sat for a few more minutes, thinking together. I was grateful she had let me into her internal world by sharing her feelings. This transition to home-learning math was a new situation for us, and it was clear she wanted to process some big feelings about it.

I told her I wanted to think more about this, and maybe she and I could come up with some way she could respond to her peers. As we sat together, an idea began to form, "I wonder…" I started. "What if you explained it by comparing it to something they'd understand?"

I continued the thought, "One analogy could be that all the students are taking music class. Most of the kids are learning to play the flute, and so flute is what they teach at school. You are also taking music class, but you are learning to play the violin. You could stay at school for music class, but since they only teach music for the flute, it wouldn't help you much. It would be much better if you could take a music class specifically for violin."

I could tell she was playing the scenario out in her mind. After some thought, she looked at me, "I like that. It makes sense too because lots of my friends are in band, so they'll get it."

Then, she sat up straight at the table, and I could see she was now ready for the math lesson.

What my daughter desired on that day was the same thing she has needed throughout her journey with dyscalculia. She needed someone to see her, accept her, and respond appropriately to her needs. "Attunement" is a term psychologists use to describe the act of being able to empathize with another and respond appropriately to their needs. Children need attunement from parents and caregivers to develop into healthy individuals. Adults also need this same experience and connection with others in their lives.

Sometimes, I am dismayed by all the change that is needed for dyscalculics to feel included and to thrive in a number-centric society. School systems need a complete remodel when it comes to providing education for dyscalculics. Governmental policies need to be created to both provide accommodations for those with learning differences and remove the current barriers to adequate assistance. Further research for dyscalculia must be funded. Above all else, societal recognition of dyscalculia is required to begin any of these changes.

It helps to remember that my responsibility is to start with the dyscalculic individual in my care—my daughter. A guiding question has been, "Are there ways I can better understand my daughter and respond to who she is with the appropriate help and guidance?" In order to help children thrive in the midst of dyscalculia, or any learning or behavioral challenge, we need to start with the foundational step of recognizing who they are, including their gifts and talents as well as their difficulties and challenges. Then, we can respond accordingly to their needs.

I have found that this process often means getting clear about what is most important for my child and our family. This clarity helps me face my internal beliefs and any history that may get in the way of responding well to my child. Responding to a neurodivergent child's needs usually requires setting aside other's perceptions about how things should be done, especially those who do not understand the child's challenge, whether dyscalculia or another difference. If we focus on what is necessary and let go of the unnecessary societal expectations or alter the ill-fitting systems, we will be well on our way to providing a safe place for our children to develop and thrive.

One way we can gain a greater understanding of our child's unique situation is through a detailed and informative private evaluation. This can pinpoint unique areas of strength as well as areas requiring specialized support. A comprehensive evaluation by a supportive and knowledgeable psychologist is of great aid when it comes to understanding your child's learning needs so that you can respond effectively and with greater confidence.

The unique experience of the dyscalculic mind can baffle the average person. The key is curiosity and patience. It will take time to learn more about the specific challenges your child faces, but it is possible to grow in your understanding and have greater insight into what will help them. The Resource list at the end of this book includes publications and links that have been instrumental in informing my own understanding of my daughter's dyscalculic mind, and I am confident they can help you as you seek knowledge of your own.

Modifying a child's educational setting is one appropriate response. It requires flexibility and creativity but may be the best way to support your child's unique wiring—even if it means using tools and materials others deem childish so that your dyscalculic learner can grasp mathematical concepts that are not accessible to them via traditional methods. It is important to remember that each child is unique and, therefore, requires an individualized learning plan; children move up and down through levels at varying speeds, and each child's learning needs should be respected.

As we learn to do the work of first seeing and responding well to our own children, we will begin to develop the capacity and awareness to notice and advocate for other dyscalculics in our community. In the end, we all benefit from a world in which we can each be seen and responded to with understanding, acceptance, and appreciation.

About the Author

Laura M. Jackson is a mom, writer, and dyscalculia advocate. She lives in the Seattle area of the Pacific Northwest. When she isn't writing about dyscalculia or supporting other parents online, she can be found spending time with her husband and two daughters. A few of her favorite things include the great outdoors, walks in the woods, gatherings with friends over a meal, good coffee, dahlias, and a set of brightly colored pens. She is also the founder of discoveringdyscalculia.com.

Notes

Chapter 3

1. The Scholars' Grove. www.thescholarsgrove.com

Chapter 4

1. Butterworth, Brian. 2019. *Dyscalculia: From Science to Education*. New York: Routledge.
2. Butterworth, Brian. *Dyscalculia*, p. 2.
3. Butterworth, Brian, and Dorian Yeo. 2004. *Dyscalculia Guidance: Helping Pupils with Specific Learning Difficulties in Maths, 1st Edition*, p. 1. London: David Fulton Publishers.
4. Butterworth, Brian. 2019. *Dyscalculia: From Science to Education*, preface p. 10 and p. 108. New York: Routledge.
5. Butterworth, Brian. 2019. *Dyscalculia*, p. 29.
6. Butterworth, Brian. 2019. *Dyscalculia*, p. 146.
7. Butterworth, Brian. 2019. *Dyscalculia*, p. 88.
8. Butterworth, Brian. 2019. *Dyscalculia*, p. 9.
9. Butterworth, Brian. 2019. *Dyscalculia*, p. 123.
10. Butterworth, Brian. 2019. *Dyscalculia*, p. 111.
11. Butterworth, Brian. 2019. *Dyscalculia*, p. 8.
12. Butterworth, Brian. 2019. *Dyscalculia*, p. 144.

Chapter 6

1. Butterworth, Brian. 2019. *Dyscalculia: From Science to Education*, p. 147. New York: Routledge.
2. Bird, Ronit. 2013. *Exploring Numbers through Dot Patterns*, p. iv. http://www.ronitbird.com/ebooks-for-learners-with-dyscalculia/#ebook1
3. Butterworth, Brian. 2019. *Dyscalculia: From Science to Education*, p. 148. New York: Routledge.
4. Bird, Ronit. 2013. *Exploring Numbers through Dot Patterns*, p. iii. http://www.ronitbird.com/ebooks-for-learners-with-dyscalculia/#ebook1

5. "An Interview with Jane Emerson—Speech and Language Therapist and Specialist SEN Teacher." 2020. http://www.educationalneuroscience.org.uk/2020/04/15

6. Bird, Ronit. 2013. *Exploring Numbers through Cuisenaire Rods*, p. 28. http://www.ronitbird.com/ebooks-for-learners-with-dyscalculia/#ebook2

7. Bird, Ronit. 2013. *Exploring Numbers through Cuisenaire Rods*, pp. iv, 2, and 9.

8. Butterworth, Brian. 2019. *Dyscalculia: From Science to Education*, pp. 47 and 146. New York: Routledge.

9. Bird, Ronit. 2013. *Exploring Numbers through Dot Patterns*, p. iv. http://www.ronitbird.com/ebooks-for-learners-with-dyscalculia/#ebook1

10. Butterworth, Brian. 2019. *Dyscalculia: From Science to Education*, pp. 47 and 146. New York: Routledge.

11. Bird, Ronit. 2013. *Exploring Numbers through Dot Patterns*, p. 12. http://www.ronitbird.com/ebooks-for-learners-with-dyscalculia/#ebook1

12. Bird, Ronit. 2013. *Exploring Numbers through Dot Patterns*, p. 13.

13. Bird, Ronit. 2013. *Exploring Numbers through Dot Patterns*, pp. 31 and 38.

14. Butterworth, Brian. 2019. *Dyscalculia: From Science to Education*, p. 149. New York: Routledge.

15. Butterworth, Brian. 2019. *Dyscalculia*, p. 149.

Chapter 7

1. Abeel, Samantha. 2005. *My Thirteenth Winter*, p. 49. New York: Scholastic.

2. Butterworth, Brian. 2019. *Dyscalculia: From Science to Education*, p. xi. New York: Routledge.

3. "1-The Reformer Enneagram Type One." The Enneagram Institute. https://www.enneagraminstitute.com/type-1

4. Bauer, Susan Wise. 2018. *Rethinking School*, pp. 25–26. New York: W. W. Norton & Company.

Chapter 8

1. Jackson, Laura. 2020. "Dyscalculia Impacts More than Just Math Class–Part 2." https://www.lauramjackson.com/blog/dyscalculia-impacts-more-than-just-math-class-part-2

2. Time Timer. https://www.timetimer.com

3. Rothmann, Line. 2015. "My World without Numbers." TEDxVennelyst-Blvd. https://youtu.be/rlPFv_EDnvY

4. Jackson, Laura. 2021. "Tips for Teachers on Class Schedules." https://www.lauramjackson.com/blog/tips-for-teachers-on-class-schedules
5. Welcome Industries. https://www.welcomeindustries.com

Chapter 9

1. Abeel, Samantha. 2005. *My Thirteenth Winter*, p. 49. New York: Scholastic.
2. Rothmann, Line. 2015. "My World without Numbers." TEDxVennelyst-Blvd. https://youtu.be/rlPFv_EDnvY
3. Butterworth, Brian. 2019. *Dyscalculia: From Science to Education*, p. 22. New York: Routledge.
4. Dyscalculia Network. www.dyscalculianetwork.com/training-courses
5. "Dyslexia thinking skills are mission critical for protecting the country." https://www.gchg.gov.uk/news/dyslexic-thinking-skills

Resources

Books

Differently Wired: A Parent's Guide to Raising an Atypical Child with Confidence and Hope by Debbie Reber (2020)

Dyscalculia: From Science to Education by Brian Butterworth (2019)

Dyscalculia Guidance: Helping Pupils with Specific Learning Difficulties in Maths by Brian Butterworth and Dorian Yeo (2004)

The Dyscalculia Resource Book: Games and Puzzles for ages 7–14 by Ronit Bird (2017)

The Dyscalculia Solution: Teaching Number Sense by Jane Emerson and Patricia Babtie (2014)

The Dyscalculia Toolkit: Supporting Learning Difficulties in Maths by Ronit Bird (2021)

Exploring Numbers through Dot Patterns, Exploring Numbers through Cuisenaire Rods, Understanding Times Tables, and *Understanding Fractions* (4 ebooks) by Ronit Bird

Gifted Myths: An Easy-to-Read Guide to the Myths, Science and History of the Gifted and Twice-Exceptional by Kathleen Humble (2019)

Helping Your Child with Language-Based Learning Disabilities: Strategies to Succeed in School and Life with Dyscalculia, Dyslexia, ADHD, and Auditory Processing Disorder by Daniel Franklin (2018)

My Thirteenth Winter: A Memoir by Samantha Abeel (2008)

Overcoming Dyscalculia and Difficulties with Numbers by Ronit Bird (2021)

Rethinking School: How to Take Charge of Your Child's Education by Susan Wise Bauer (2019)

To Be Gifted and Learning Disabled: Strength-Based Strategies for Helping Twice-Exceptional Students With LD, ADHD, ASD, and More by Susan Baum (2017)

Understanding Dyscalculia and Numeracy Difficulties: A Guide for Parents, Teachers and Other Professionals by Patricia Babtie and Jane Emerson (2015)

Websites

Ronit Bird: www.ronitbird.com

Discovering Dyscalculia: www.discoveringdyscalculia.com

Dyscalculia Network: www.dyscalculianetwork.com

Dyscalculia Services: dyscalculiaservices.com

Emerson House Learning: www.emersonhouse.co.uk

Understood: www.understood.org